SELECTED EXCERPTS FROM THE
BUDDHIST WRITINGS
OF THE VENERABLE

Xiao Pingshi

Also by the Venerable Xiao Pingshi

The Correct Meanings of the Āgamas: Exploring the Origin of the Consciousness-Only Doctrine (7 vol.)
《阿含正義—唯識學探源》

An Exposition on the Laṅkāvatāra Sūtra (10 vol.)
《楞伽經詳解》

A Discourse on the Śūraṅgama Sūtra (15 vol.)
《楞嚴經講記》

A Discourse on the Vimalakīrti Sūtra (6 vol.)
《維摩詰經講記》

Mastering the Essence of the Diamond Sūtra (9 vol.)
《金剛經宗通》

The Secret Meanings of the Heart Sūtra
《心經密意》

Perfect Harmony between Chan and Pure Land
《禪淨圓融》

Chan: Before and After Enlightenment
《禪—悟前與悟後》

The True versus the False Enlightenment
《真假開悟》

The Undeniable Existence of the Tathāgatagarbha
《真實如來藏》

Mastering and Skillfully Articulating the Essence of Buddhist Enlightenment: The Way to Buddhahood
《宗通與說通—成佛之道》

Signless Buddha-Mindfulness
《無相念佛》

Wrong Views versus the Buddha Dharma
《邪見與佛法》

The Seventh and Eighth Mental Consciousnesses? The Supra-Consciousness that Transcends Time and Space
《第七意識與第八意識？—穿越時空「超意識」》

Behind the Façade of Tibetan Tantra (4 vol.)
《狂密與真密》

SELECTED EXCERPTS FROM THE
BUDDHIST WRITINGS
OF THE VENERABLE

Xiao Pingshi

Translated by
the English Translation Team of the True
Enlightenment Education Foundation

Wholesome Vision™

Selected Excerpts from the Buddhist Writings of the Venerable Xiao Pingshi
Copyright © 2016 by Wholesome Vision™
Published by Wholesome Vision™

30 N Gould St, Ste N

Sheridan, WY 82801

USA

WholesomeVision.com
Enlighten.org.tw

All Rights Reserved. No part of this work may be reproduced, scanned, or distributed in any printed or electronic form without written permission of the publisher.

ISBN:978-1-945892-32-5

First U.S. Edition

ABOUT THE AUTHOR

Born in 1944, the Venerable Master Xiao Pingshi (蕭平實) was raised in a farming family in central Taiwan. Seeking answers to the truth of human existence, he became a committed Buddhist disciple and practitioner in his forties, and in 1990 attained awakening to the True Mind via Chan contemplation and the aid of an incredible Dharma-door called "signless Buddha-mindfulness."

In 1997, Master Xiao established the Buddhist True Enlightenment Practitioners Association in order to offer different levels of Dharma classes to practitioners. Presently, the Association's practice centers have reached all major cities of Taiwan, and beyond to Hong Kong and the United States. Since the founding of the Association, Master Xiao has been giving weekly lectures on important Buddhist scriptures, such as the *Laṅkāvatāra Sūtra,* the *Śūraṅgama Sūtra,* the *Sūtra on Upāsaka Precepts,* the *Śrīmālādevī Siṃhanāda Sūtra,* the *Diamond Sūtra,* the *Lotus Sūtra,* and so forth.

To elucidate the Buddha Dharma and its stages of cultivation for all interested learners, Master Xiao has also published more than a hundred books on a wide range of Buddhist subjects. These include the combined cultivation of Chan and Pure Land, the realization of the Path to Liberation expounded in the *Āgamas,* the analysis of the profound Middle-Way teachings and the exegesis of key Consciousness-Only scriptures. All of his books emphasize the points that Buddhism is a path of personal realization and that realization can only come through a continual process of listening to, contemplating, and actually practicing the Buddha Dharma.

Contents

SELECTED EXCERPTS FROM THE BUDDHIST WRITINGS OF THE VENERABLE XIAO PINGSHI

EDITOR'S INTRODUCTION 1
Part I: Preface to *Signless Buddha-Mindfulness* 11
Part II: Preface to *The Contemplation of Non-Self in Mahāyāna Buddhism* 19
Part III: Foreword to *The Real and the Deluded Practitioners of Chan* 28
Part IV: Excerpts from *Behind the Façade of Tibetan Tantra* 40
Part V: Excerpts from *The Essence of Buddhist Enlightenment: The Awakened Eye* 47

《平實導師法語選輯》[CHINESE VERSION]

編輯序言 65
一、《無相念佛》自序 71
二、《大乘無我觀》序言 75
三、《真假禪和》前言 79
四、《狂密與真密》選錄 84
五、《宗門道眼》選錄 87

CHART: The Cultivation Stages within the Two Main Paths of Buddha Bodhi 95

佛菩提二主要道次第概要表 100

EDITOR'S INTRODUCTION

Two thousand and five hundred years after its inception in India, today Buddhism has spread to every continent. In spite of its global presence, Buddhism in our modern world has often been reduced to shallow pursuits due to the difficulty for Buddhist practitioners to comprehend its essence. For the same reason, the practices essential to the actual realization of Buddha Dharma have also been distorted to a point that they now contradict the Buddha's teachings. So, is Buddhism only about doing good deeds? Letting go of craving? Seeking peace and lasting happiness? Taming the mind with meditation? In his lucid discourses on the Buddha Dharma, Master Xiao Pingshi systematically demonstrates that, while the teachings of Buddha Śākyamuni encompass all secular efforts and practices, the core teaching of the Dharma resides precisely in the transcendental realization of the True Mind—the origin of the universe and all existence. Indeed, it was the possession and command of all mundane and supramundane knowledge that earned Buddha Śākyamuni the exalted epithets, including "the one with perfect and complete enlightenment," "the knower of the mundane world," and "the supreme teacher of humans and celestial beings."

Secularization aside, in modern times Buddhism has often been stripped of its actual practice and relegated to purely academic studies. Alarmed by this trend, from the outset when he began teaching, Master Xiao has always emphasized the actual realization of the Buddha Dharma, which is attained through two components: first, accurate understanding of the Buddha's teachings; second, correct practice methods clearly defined by cultivation stages spoken of by the Buddha. To help Buddhist learners gain wisdom that they can apply in everyday life, and even realize the ultimate reality of our existence, he designed three levels of courses that integrate knowledge and practice. Among the three, the first two elementary and intermediate courses impart the fundamentals of the Buddha Dharma—including the cultivation of the six *pāramitās*—as well as effective ways to develop the power of in-motion meditative concentration, which is essential for Chan contemplation that leads to the actual realization of the True Mind. In his advanced course for students who have realized the True Mind, Master Xiao teaches *prajñā* (the wisdom regarding the ultimate reality), the materials for the stages before the First Ground, as well as the contents of deeper cultivation, the materials for the stages above the First Ground.

Above all, Buddhist cultivation must be grounded in both accurate understanding and actual realization of the Buddha's teachings. However, it must be noted that actual realization should not be regarded as just theoretical understanding, for theoretical understanding alone without actual realization often leads to faulty conclusions. To help Buddhist learners acquire an in-depth comprehension of the Buddha's profound discourses, Master Xiao has written extensive commentaries on key scriptures of the Three Vehicles of Buddhism, including *An Exposition on the Laṅkāvatāra Sūtra*, *The Secret Meanings of the Heart Sūtra*, *The Correct Meanings of the Āgamas*, *A Discourse of the Śūraṅgama Sūtra*, *A Discourse on the Śrīmālādevī Siṃhanāda Sūtra*, *Mastering the Essence of the Diamond Sūtra*, *A Discourse on the Vimalakīrti Sūtra*, *A Discourse on the Sūtra on Upāsaka Precepts*, among many others. In addition to scriptural expositions, Master Xiao has authored many titles on a range of Buddhist topics, in which he introduces practitioners to effective practice methods and dispels widespread misconceptions that bedevil them. These titles include *Signless Buddha-Mindfulness*, *Stages in Cultivating Buddha-Mindfulness Samādhi*, *The True versus the False Enlightenment*, *Perfect Harmony between Chan and Pure Land*, *The Undeniable Existence of the Tathāgatagarbha*, the seven-part series of *Critiques and Commentaries on Gong'ans*, and the four-volume *Behind the Façade of Tibetan Tantra*.

Master Xiao's interpretation and instruction of the Dharma have prodded contemporary practitioners and scholars to re-examine their fundamental understanding of Buddhism, evidenced by numerous publications discussing his views. Going beyond the literal meaning of the scriptures, he delves into the true import of the Buddha's edification, delineates the complete cultivation stages of the Buddha Dharma, and provides penetrating answers with clarity to some of the most sought-after questions concerning the Buddha Dharma:

❖ According to the teachings of the *Āgamas*, does the transmission of karmic content across lifetimes and the realization of the Path of Liberation require the existence of an eternal mind?

- ❖ What is the doctrinal thread that ties the teachings of the Three Vehicles of Buddha Dharma into a unifying whole?
- ❖ Between the teachings delivered in the second and the third turning of the Dharma Wheel by Buddha Śākyamuni, which is the superior and ultimate?
- ❖ Did the Buddha set forth an ontological system of six consciousnesses or eight consciousnesses?
- ❖ Did the Buddha deny the presence of any eternal entity as the ontic essence of phenomenal existence?
- ❖ How does one acquire the level of meditative concentration necessary for guarding a *huatou* or contemplating a *gong'an*, the two pedagogical devices used in the Chan tradition, to catalyze awakening—the direct realization of the True Mind?
- ❖ Is the awakening in the Chinese Chan tradition really attainable and verifiable?
- ❖ What is the essence of awakening? What are the stages of cultivation after attaining awakening?
- ❖ Does achieving a thoughtless mental state through meditation mean awakening?
- ❖ Are the teachings of Tibetan tantric "Buddhism" (a.k.a. Tibetan Tantrism, esoteric Buddhism, or Lamaism) in line with the Buddha's teachings of the Three Vehicles?

Substantiating his arguments with scriptural references and firsthand experience from rigorous practice, Master Xiao proves in his writings that:

- The teachings of Buddha Śākyamuni are not conceptually abstract theories but experientially verifiable truths.
- The Three Vehicles of Buddha Dharma are progressive and integrated teachings founded upon the True Mind, also known in the scriptures as the *tathāgatagarbha*. The existence of the *tathāgatagarbha* is taught implicitly in the passages about "rebirth-consciousness" and in those about "the ten links of dependent arising" in the *Āgamas* and *Nikāyas*. Endowed with immeasurable attributes, the *tathāgatagarbha* is the matrix carrying karmic seeds and substantiating transmigration within the six paths of rebirth.
- Buddha Śākyamuni taught an ontological system of eight consciousnesses: the five sensory consciousnesses, the mental consciousness, the *manas* (the seventh consciousness), and the foundational consciousness (the ālaya-consciousness, or the eighth consciousness). These eight consciousness are responsible for the arising of all mundane and supramundane phenomena. The statement that "the three realms are manifestation of mind, while all phenomena owe their existence to consciousnesses," found in the *Avataṃsaka Sūtra,* is a truth that can be directly realized and ascertained.
- The True Mind—which is known in the scriptures by a variety of names, including the *tathāgatagarbha*, the

ālaya-consciousness, the eighth consciousness, the true suchness (*bhūtatathatā;*), the signless mind, and Emptiness (*śūnyatā*)—is the mind entity that a practitioner seeks to realize via Chan contemplation. It is the essence of "Emptiness" mentioned in Buddhist scriptures and is a true existence that can be experientially verified; it is not an imagined idea or a mere conceptual designation.

❖ Among the teachings delivered in the three turnings of the Dharma Wheel, the Consciousness-Only doctrines regarding the cultivation of the knowledge-of-all-aspects (*sarvākārajñatā*) set forth in the third turning are the most profound.

❖ Until a practitioner has fulfilled the requisite cultivation of the six *pāramitās*, namely, giving, morality, forbearance, diligence, meditative concentration, and *prajñā*, he will not be able to realize the *tathāgatagarbha*.

❖ The direct realization of the *tathāgatagarbha* is the most fundamental and pivotal stage on the Bodhisattva Path, for only when a practitioner has attained such realization and does not retrogress from it is he considered to have attained a clear vision of the path to Buddhahood. Such a practitioner, however, still has a long way to go before reaching the First Ground, and still has innumerable Dharma-doors to cultivate before he can attain the ultimate fruition of Buddhahood.

❖ All realizations of the Great Vehicle and the Two Vehicles, are considered genuine only if they are supported by a commensurate level of meditative concentration.

❖ The sexual practice of Highest Yoga Tantra cannot lead to the realization of the *tathāgatagarbha*. What this practice can "realize" is confined either within the mental consciousness alone or within the combination of the first six of the eight consciousnesses. In addition, the practices of the "stage of generation" and "stage of completion" in Highest Yoga Tantra stand in complete opposition to the principles of cultivation set forth in the Three Vehicles of Buddhism.

❖ The philosophy of Prāsaṅgika Madhyamaka, espoused by Candrakīrti, Tsongkhapa, and contemporary Buddhist "masters" such as Yin-shun (印順) is in essence a theory of dependent origination without a fundamental cause. It contradicts the Buddha's teaching of the *tathāgatagarbha*, which affirms that the *tathāgatagarbha* is the everlasting and truly existent ultimate reality upon which the dependent origination of all phenomena is grounded.

This book is meant to be a sample of Master Xiao's writings on the topics that are most relevant to Buddhist practitioners in today's world. It is structured in five parts:

I. **Preface to *Signless Buddha-Mindfulness***: His first book, *Signless Buddha-Mindfulness,* introduces an entry-level practice of Bodhisattva Mahāsthāmaprāpta's Dharma-door for "perfect mastery through Buddha-mindfulness," as discussed in the *Śūraṅgama Sūtra*. In the preface, he gives a brief account of how he gained the power of in-motion meditation concentration and achieved awakening by using this highly effective and convenient Dharma-door.

II. **Preface to *The Contemplation of Non-Self in Mahāyāna Buddhism*:** This preface delves into the content of and the relationship among the awakening to the *tathāgatagarbha*, the activation of *prajñā*, and the advanced cultivation of the knowledge-of-all-aspects in the Great Vehicle.

III. **Foreword to *The Real versus the Deluded Practitioners of Chan*:** A person's awakening to the essence of the Buddha Dharma (the True Mind) ought to be consistent with the Buddha's teachings. Only after one has awakened to the True Mind and realized its inherent non-discrimination can one proceed to cultivate the knowledge-of-all-aspects, the insights essential to the attainment of Buddhahood.

IV. **Quotes from *Behind the Façade of Tibetan Tantra*:** The tantric practices in Tibetan "Buddhism" cannot bring one to attain even the first of the four fruitions in the Path to Liberation, let alone achieve the awakening in the Bodhisattva Path. On the contrary, these practices entrench both the erroneous view of self and the attachment to what belongs to self. All practice methods in Tibetan "Buddhism" such as the visualization of meditational deities (*yidams*) or the sexual tantras, fall within the scope of the first six consciousnesses rather than that of the inherently non-discriminating True Mind. As a result of this misdirection, the practitioners of Tibetan "Buddhism" cannot even embark upon the cultivation of the Three Vehicles.

V. **Quotes from *The Essence of Buddhist Enlightenment: The Awakened Eye*:** Buddhahood has to be accomplished through stage-by-stage cultivation, spanning three immeasurable eons, with the awakening to the True Mind being the most critical stage. The True Mind refers to the *tathāgatagarbha*, literally the "matrix of Buddhahood," which exhibits the inherent nature of emptiness; it is not our mental consciousness and cannot be realized by maintaining the conscious mind in any particular mental state. Only those who have realized the True Mind can understand the exact meaning and the true intent of the *gong'ans* of the Chan school.

Though sampling only a tiny section of Master Xiao's bibliographic repertoire, this book reveals insights into Buddhist teachings unseen in contemporary Buddhist literature. Whether you are a Buddhist practitioner, scholar, or just someone who is interested in knowing more about Buddhism, I invite you to look into his writings, mentioned in this book and beyond, to see the splendor of the Truth imparted by the Buddha, well-explained by Master Xiao's clear logic and friendly language.

Part I.
Preface to *Signless Buddha-Mindfulness*

For most Buddhist learners, the term "Buddha-mindfulness" simply means the recitation of the sacred name of a particular Buddha or bodhisattva. With utmost faith, as well as continuous recitation, practitioners take refuge in Buddhas and bodhisattvas, hoping to obtain a connection with them either through subtle responses or visual manifestations. While most practitioners of Buddha-mindfulness recites the name of Buddha Amitābha, Buddha Amitābha's Pure Land of Ultimate Bliss is far from being *the* only pure land. There are countless pure lands manifested by Buddhas in the worlds of ten directions, including that of our Fundamental Teacher—Buddha Śākyamuni. A distinction should also be made between the Mind-Only Pure Land and the pure lands manifested by various Buddhas.

In a broad sense, all cultivation methods of Mahāyāna Buddhism fall within the scope of the Pure Land school's Dharma-door of Buddha-mindfulness, including well-known practices such as recitation of Buddha's name, mantra chanting, prostration, offering making, tranquility and insight meditation (*samathavipaśyanā*), and observance of the precepts, as well as the chanting, copying, studying, expounding, reflecting on, and contemplating of sūtras. They are all geared toward learning the practices of Buddha, understanding the Dharma, attaining liberation, acquiring the meritorious qualities of Buddha, and ultimately, realizing the four types of pure land upon the attainment of Buddhahood.

The Pure Land tradition shares a close connection with the Chan school. To attain Buddhahood, a Pure Land practitioner cannot simply recite Buddha's name, but must draw upon the power of meditative concentration (*samādhi*) to attain direct preception of the True Mind. The realization of the True Mind marks the entering into the Path of Vision[1] on the Bodhisattva Path, whereupon one can swiftly advance to the Path of Cultivation and bring within sight the eventual attainment of Buddhahood. However, to realize the True Mind, one must practice either Chan contemplation or the tranquility and insight meditation, specifically, the method of "contemplation of principle."[2] Both of these methods

---

[1] The Bodhisattva Path is comprised of a total of fifty-two stages, divided into five progressive Paths according to the Yogācāra teaching: Accumulation, Preparation, Vision, Cultivation, and Ultimate Realization. The Path of Vision begins at the stage of Seventh Abiding and continues through to the initial phase of the First Ground. Before a practitioner can reach the Path of Vision, he or she has to make it through the Path of Accumulation and the Path of Preparation, and also directly realize the True Mind—the ultimate reality of all phenomena. For details, please refer to the chart of "The Cultivation Stages of the Two Paths within the Buddha Bodhi" at the back of this book.

[2] Chan contemplation stresses direct realization of the True Mind without relying on scriptural study. In contrast, the "contemplation of principle (*liguan* 理觀)" employs the tranquility and insight meditation as its means

call for a sufficient degree of meditative concentration, especially the ability to maintain meditative concentration while in physical motion.

The power of meditative concentration is highly essential to an adherent of the Pure Land tradition. If a Pure Land practitioner can practice the recitation of Buddha's name in conjunction with the prostration to Buddha as expedient techniques to build up his power of meditative concentration, he could easily train his mind to one-pointedness and enter Bodhisattva Mahāsthāmaprāpta's Dharma-door for "perfect mastery through Buddha-mindfulness,"[3] an accomplishment that will help secure rebirth in the Pure Land of Ultimate Bliss. Alternatively, equipped with a decent power of meditative concentration, this practitioner may also choose to proceed to the practice of contemplative Buddha-mindfulness, through which he could "spontaneously awaken to the True Mind without employing skillful means," as stated in the *Śūraṅgama Sūtra*. If, instead, this practitioner applies his power of meditative concentration gained from the entry practice of Bodhisattva Mahāsthāmaprāpta's Dharma-door of Buddha-mindfulness toward Chan contemplation, he could also awaken to the True Mind as

---

and relies on the reflection and investigation of the principle of emptiness or suchness—the nature of the True Mind—expounded in the scriptures to achieve direct realization of the ultimate reality.

[3] Bodhisattva Mahāsthāmaprāpta's Dharma-door for "perfect mastery through Buddha-mindfulness" is a method of signless mindfulness of Buddha illustrated in the *Śūraṅgama Sūtra*. Please note that the signless mindfulness introduced in this book is only the entry-level practice of the Bodhisattva Mahāsthāmaprāpta's profound Dharma-door.

the "gateless gate" will reveal itself spontaneously. This is how the practice of Pure Land crosses over to Chan.

In other words, if a Buddhist disciple cultivates the Dharma-door of the Pure Land following the essentials of samādhi cultivation, and uses the Pure Land methods to enhance his power of in-motion meditative concentration, he can make quick and equal progress in both Chan and Pure Land practices. I humbly put forth the above views for the sole purpose of benefiting all readers.

I would like to give a brief account of the events that led up to the writing of this book. At the beginning of 1987, my hectic work schedule allowed me no time for meditation at all. Every evening, I was extremely weary during my recitation of the *Diamond Sūtra*, and I usually concluded this daily routine with prostrations to the Buddha immediately after.

One summer evening that year, as I was prostrating to the Buddha, it suddenly occurred to me that I should drop the name and image of Buddha, and instead hold only a pure thought of Buddha during prostration. I tried it out right away. From that day on, I started to make prostrations while bearing only a thought of Buddha, a method I have since termed "signless Buddha-mindfulness." As time went on, I became proficient in this practice. I was filled with Dharma-joy and was impermeable to the stress and fatigue of worldly living. Deriving so much joy from this practice, I even ceased my old evening routine, focusing instead on prostration with signless mindfulness of Buddha. During the rest of the day's activities, I held a signless pure thought of Buddha in mind.

By the end of 1988, I wanted to share my Dharma-joy with fellow practitioners. I started to sift through my memory and jotted down every step I had taken to accomplish my practice. At the same time, I scoured and reviewed sūtras and treatises to locate scriptural verification of my method. Right before completing my writing, I came upon the section "Bodhisattva Mahāsthāmaprāpta's Dharma-door for Perfect Mastery through Buddha-Mindfulness" in the *Śūraṅgama Sūtra*. I was elated when my eyes set upon the words "recollect and be mindful of Buddha." As I read on and saw, "rein in all six sense faculties and abide in one continuous pure thought to enter samādhi," I realized that my method was precisely the Dharma-door "of perfect mastery through Buddha-mindfulness" illustrated by Bodhisattva Mahāsthāmaprāpta.

In April 1989, I compiled my notes into a short essay, entitled "A Discussion of Signless Buddha-Prostration and Buddha-Mindfulness." After I finished the draft of this article, I came upon the writings of the Venerable Xuyun (虛雲和尚), and finally acquired a clear understanding of the principle and method of the guarding of a *huatou*.[4] Only then did I realize that, while I thought I was contemplating *huatou* and boldly claimed that I was doing so, I had been merely uttering words and observing their trail.

Why was I not able to contemplate *huatou* in my earlier attempts? It was simple: at the beginning, I didn't have the ability

---

[4] *Huatou* 話頭: literally "word head," *huatou* refers to what comes before words. It should be noted that while *hua* means spoken words in Chinese, in the Chan context it should be understood as a thought or idea associated with linguistic contents or images. *Huatou*, therefore, refers to the wordless and imageless awareness preceding the formation of a thought. In the Chan school, the guarding and contemplation of *huatou* is a pedagogical device used to help practitioners uncover the True Mind.

to maintain a focused mind in motion. Only after I mastered the signless mindfulness of Buddha was I able to maintain a focused mind in motion, and hence to contemplate *huatou*.

In the afternoon of August 6, 1989, I twice entered into a state of "seeing the mountain as not being mountain" during a group practice and experienced for the first time the state of the "dark barrel."[5] After that, I wavered in and out of a mass of doubt. In early November of 1989, I decided to close my business and focus on Chan contemplation at home after I returned from a pilgrimage to India and Nepal. Around four o'clock in the afternoon of the second day of the eleventh lunar month in 1990, I broke free of the "dark barrel" and my striving in Chan contemplation finally ended.

In retrospect, I realized that the root cause of most practitioners' lack of progress in their Dharma cultivation is the inability to maintain meditative concentration in motion. This book was written to help practitioners swiftly attain an undisturbed mind during their practice of Buddha-mindfulness. Once they develop this skill, they can quickly move on to the contemplation of *huatou* and *gong'an*.[6]

---

[5] The "dark barrel" refers to a state during Chan contemplation when one is so single-mindedly focused on the contemplation that one becomes oblivious to the external environment. At this point, the practitioner has not directly realized the True Mind.

[6] *Gong'an* 公案: this term, known as *koan* in Japanese, carries the literal meaning of "public case" or "precedent." A *gong'an* in the Chan tradition typically consists of dialogues between a Chan master and his disciple(s). Like *huatou*, a Chan practitioner is supposed to contemplate the meaning of *gong'an* without using any language or image in order to achieve sudden awakening to the True Mind.

At the request of fellow practitioners, I gave a lecture on signless Buddha-mindfulness—the expedient way to enter Bodhisattva Mahāsthāmaprāpta's Dharma-door for "perfect mastery through Buddha-mindfulness"—once a week for three consecutive weeks beginning on September 3, 1991. These three lectures were held at the Chan center of the Buddhist society of a financial institution and at the Chens' residence in Shipai, both located in Taipei.

There were thirty people in these two practice groups at the time. Most of them used recitation of Buddha's name as their practice method. By putting what they had learned from my lectures into practice, two of them were able to accomplish signless Buddha-mindfulness within a mere six weeks. After three months, six people had mastered this practice. As of today (February 28, 1992),[7] thirteen people have mastered it less than six months. Still more people are joining in and making speedy progress. The rate of mastery and the speed of progress are very encouraging. Excluding those who did not practice prostration due to individual conditions, the main reason for the others' lack of progress was their aversion to this method and its preparatory expedient—namely, the recitation of Buddha's name. When they finally changed their minds after seeing that those who had mastered this method were starting to guard *huatou* and contemplate Chan, they were already three to four months behind.

These results and observations excited me greatly. They showed that signless Buddha-mindfulness could definitely be mastered

---

[7] This book was originally written in Chinese and was first published in Taiwan in 1993.

when facilitated by appropriate methods and practiced with continuous diligence. A feeling of compassion welled up from within, compassion that cannot bear to see the decline of the holy teachings and does not wish that sentient beings suffer, and so I made haste to complete the writing of this book during the winter break. My writing is far from elegant, but I try to articulate myself clearly and coherently. For easy comprehension, I wrote in a colloquial, direct, and somewhat repetitive style to get my points across. May all Buddhist practitioners master signless Buddha-mindfulness, be filled with Dharma-joy, spread this method to benefit countless beings, and enter the Ocean of the Vairocana Nature.

Take refuge in our Fundamental Teacher Buddha Śākyamuni
Take refuge in Bodhisattva Avalokiteśvara of Great Compassion
Take refuge in Bodhisattva Mahāsthāmaprāpta

Xiao Pingshi
A disciple of the Three Jewels
Feb 28, 1992

Part II.

Preface to *The Contemplation of Non-Self in Mahāyāna Buddhism*

The way to Buddhahood is only found in the Great Vehicle. It is absent in the Two Vehicles; it is unknown to the disciples of the Two Vehicles. The Two Vehicles are limited to the observation and contemplation of phenomenal existence—the aggregates (*skandha*), sense-fields (*āyatana*), and elements (*dhātu*). Their cultivation primarily uses the Four Foundations of Mindfulness to realize the Four Noble Truths, the Noble Eightfold Path, and the Twelve Links of Dependent Origination. The Buddha does implicitly touch upon the ultimate reality (the essence of "nirvana without remainder") that underlies these phenomenal existence in his teachings of the Two Vehicles. However, the disciples of the Two Vehicles—whether learners or adepts—have no insight into it. Only when they decide to aspire to the Great Vehicle will the Buddha help them realize the ultimate reality, by which they could become great bodhisattvas in the Great Vehicle.

In this Dharma-ending era, the teachings about the way to Buddhahood have already been lost in most of the places, and the

Buddhist "masters" of our time no longer have proper knowledge of them. A case in point is Buddhist master Yin-shun. In *The Way to Buddhahood*, he presents teachings that deviate from, or are irrelevant to, the correct cultivation of Buddhahood as taught by Buddha Śākyamuni. On close examination of his doctrinal position, it is apparent that Yin-shun was essentially a proponent of the Prāsaṅgika Madhyamaka philosophy[8] espoused by the Gelug sect of Tibetan Lamaism.[9] This philosophy is a form of nihilism grounded in the theory that all phenomena are interdependently originated without the need for a fundamental cause. It is an idea born out of speculation and is at odds with the correct cultivation of Buddhahood.

The cultivation central to the attainment of Buddhahood is the realization of the knowledge-of-all-aspects (*sarvākārajñatā*)—the knowledge of the fundamental mind and the various kinds of functional seeds (*bīja*) stored in it. This mind of ultimate reality, also known as the eighth consciousness or the *tathāgatagarbha*,

---

[8] Prāsaṅgika Madhyamaka: The "Middle Way" philosophy proposed by Buddhapālita in the fourth century. Since it asserts that all phenomenal existences originate interdependently without a fundamental cause and denies the existence of the eighth consciousness (a.k.a. the *tathāgatagarbha* or the ālaya-consciousness), the origin of all phenomenal existences, it contradicts the Middle Way view established on the nature of the *tathāgatagarbha*, set forth in the sacred teachings of Buddha Śākyamuni.

[9] Tibetan Lamaism: refers to the four most prominent sects of Tibetan Lamaism—Nyingma, Kagyu, Sakya, and Gelug—which are inaccurately known to the world as Tibetan "Buddhism." The Jonang tradition that appeared in Tibet from the twelfth to seventeenth century, however, should be regarded as the real Tibetan Buddhism because its doctrine of "other-emptiness" is consistent with Buddha Śākyamuni's teachings.

is the origin or "first cause" of all phenomena. Together, this fundamental mind and the immeasurable seeds it contains bring into existence the five aggregates, the twelve sense-fields, and the eighteen elements that constitute a sentient being. After a sentient being's eighteen elements have been fully generated, they further interact with the seeds in the fundamental mind to directly and indirectly produce all ordinary or noble phenomena within the ten realms of reality (*dharmadhātu*),[10] which in turn make all kinds of supramundane unconditioned (*asaṃskṛta*) dharmas shown. Thus, it is said that the ultimate reality of all phenomena is this uncreated and self-existing fundamental mind called the *tathāgatagarbha*.

Every sentient being owes his or her existence to his own *tathāgatagarbha*, which before awakening is given the name "ālaya-consciousness." The ālaya-consciousness is precisely the eighth consciousness, or the true suchness, to which all enlightened Chan practitioners have awakened.[11]

---

[10] The ten realms of reality refer to the ten categories of sentient existence in Buddhist cosmology: the realms of hell beings, hungry ghosts, animals, demigods (*asura*), humans, celestial beings, hearers (*śrāvaka*), solitary-realizers (*pratyekabuddha*), and Buddhas.

[11] In Vol. 4 of the *Record of the Mirror of the Source* (*Zongjing lu* 宗鏡錄; T48, no. 2016, 435a4-7), Chan master Yongming Yanshou (永明延壽) writes: "The *Laṅkāvatāra Sūtra* states that, 'The *tathāgatagarbha* is called the ālaya-consciousness; it is permanent and unceasing, and like the ocean and its waves, it coexists with ignorance and the seven consciousnesses.' It also says: "The *tathāgatagarbha* has been impregnated with deluded and unwholesome habits since beginningless time, and is thus called the repository consciousness.' Those who have realized that all phenomena can be ascribed to this original mind are said to have attained direct

Since ancient times, there have always been Chan practitioners who declare that "awakening means immediate attainment of the ultimate Buddhahood" soon after they have attained direct realization of the ālaya-consciousness. These newly enlightened practitioners have not developed thorough understanding of the way to Buddhahood. They made this presumptuous and lofty statement because they unwisely bought into the views of those whose awakening was either false or shallow, and furthermore, failed to explore why in the sūtras many great bodhisattvas do not attain Buddhahood immediately after awakening to the ālaya-consciousness. As a result, they fell prey to what is called "wild Chan."[12] The deviant discourses they disseminated misled Buddhist learners of both their own time and the present day.

Practitioners fall victim to "wild Chan" usually for the following reasons: (1) they do not truly understand the content of Chan awakening and how this awakening should be positioned with respect to the cultivation sequence of *prajñā* (the wisdom regarding the ultimate reality); (2) they do not understand that the scriptural teachings associated with the third turning of the Dharma Wheel are discourses on the higher knowledge (*adhiprajñaśikṣ*ā), i.e., the knowledge-of-all-aspects, undertaken by enlightened bodhisattvas on or above the First Ground of the Bodhisattva Path; (3) their

---

comprehension of the ultimate truth and will thereupon attain liberation."
楞伽經云,如來藏名阿賴耶識,而與無明七識共俱,如大海波,常不斷絕。又云: 如來藏者,為無始虛偽惡習所熏,名為識藏。若此一心,推末歸本者, 謂證第一義,則得解脫。

[12] Wild Chan (*kuangchan* 狂禪): the wild overestimation of one's attainment of awakening and Dharma knowledge.

understanding about the stages of cultivation in the Bodhisattva Path is incorrect; and (4) they are unable to comprehend and realize the Buddha's implicit teachings of the ultimate reality in the *Āgamas*. In consequence, they adopted erroneous exegesis such as that of Yin-shun's of the *Āgamas*,[13] became beguiled by the Prāsaṅgika Madhyamaka philosophy promoted by Tibetan "Buddhism," or even became avid supporters of the propagation of the Prāsaṅgika Madhyamaka. In doing so, they unknowingly commit the extremely grievous sin of undermining the Buddha Dharma—all the while believing that they are protecting and spreading it.

To guard against wild Chan and its undesirable consequences, a Buddhist practitioner should understand that while attaining Chan awakening is highly important, it is equally crucial to acquire thorough understanding of the content of Chan awakening, and to which stage this awakening corresponds on the Bodhisattva Path. In the Great-Vehicle cultivation of *prajñā*, Chan awakening corresponds only to the initial phase of the Path of Vision; it is a long way before the First Ground on the Bodhisattva Path, where proficient comprehension of *prajñā* is attained. Therefore, after attaining awakening, a practitioner with this understanding will begin to explore the cultivation he needs to undertake to advance toward Buddhahood. He will study the sūtras and eventually pore over the Consciousness-Only scriptures explicated during the third turning of the Dharma Wheel. With earnest investigation,

---

[13] For details, please refer to *The Correct Meanings of the Āgamas* (*A han zhengyi* 阿含正義) by Xiao Pingshi (Taipei: True Wisdom Publishing Center, 2006).

he will gradually learn about the correct sequence of cultivation on the Bodhisattva Path and eventually reach the First Ground, also known as the "stage of proficiency."

Once the practitioner has reached the First Ground, he will be able to competently undertake the works of the Buddha's lineage. He will devote himself to the refutation of incorrect doctrines by contrasting them with the authentic Dharma, thus reviving the Buddha Dharma and abiding as a true "Buddha's son." A First-Ground bodhisattva will take in more profound knowledge-of-the-aspects-of-paths (*mārgakārajñatā*). Equipped with more profound knowledge-of-the-aspects-of-paths, he is able to deliver all sentient beings from suffering and ignorance, refute specious views among some Buddhists, and set Buddhist learners on the right course of cultivation. Thus, the Buddha's teachings will be upheld and protected.

Moreover, bodhisattvas who have entered the First Ground are able to thoroughly comprehend the teachings of the Path to Liberation of the Two Vehicles. They can correctly expound the cultivation of the Two Vehicles and guide their practitioners to attain the fruitions of liberation. The realization of these fruitions will arouse great aspirations in practitioners of the Two Vehicles, who will then be able to overcome their fears of cyclical birth-and-death, and be willing to commit themselves to the deliverance of sentient beings in endless time to come. A First-Ground bodhisattva is also able to rectify misunderstandings about the Great Vehicle that are often held by adherents of the Two Vehicles, and in doing so steer them to the Great Vehicle.

It must be stressed, however, that none of such extraordinary accomplishments are possible without first attaining Chan awakening and undergoing the subsequent practice of the "contemplation of non-self" during the Three Stages of Worthiness[14] and on the ten Grounds along the Bodhisattva Path. It is the direct comprehension of non-self attained at each of these cultivation stages that enables a bodhisattva to expound and distinguish the "contemplation of non-self" in the Great Vehicle from the "contemplation of no-self" in the Two Vehicles. The delineation of the contemplation of non-self in the Great Vehicle enhances the *prajñā* of enlightened Buddhist disciples and helps unenlightened disciples recognize and abandon the wrong views they have acquired from those who treat the Buddha Dharma as a research subject instead of engaging in actual practice. Given the weighty significance of the contemplation of non-self in the Great Vehicle, this book was written to impart a clear understanding of the subject for both enlightened and unenlightened Buddhist disciples.

This book traces its origin to an invitation I received from Chairman Hou of Tainan Spinning Company to tour the Hou's Ancestral Shrine. During the visit, I was asked to speak about the Buddha Dharma. This speech given at the Hou's Ancestral Shrine in the Beimen Village of Tainan formed the basis of this book. I had no plan to give any kind of lecture of the Buddha Dharma on that particular occasion, and my agreeing to it was due to the

---

[14] The Three Stages of Worthiness (*sanxian wei* 三賢位) refer to the ten stages of Abiding, Practice, and Dedication on the Bodhisattva Path.

suggestion of my fellow practitioners. Since I had witnessed the confusion surrounding the sequence of cultivation on the path to Buddhahood, I came up with the topic of my speech in a rather impromptu fashion. My fellow practitioners from Tainan spread the news of my coming lecture in the greater Tainan area and made this Dharma gathering happen.

Swamped with engagements before the speech, I had no time to draft an outline. Because of this, I spoke in a very casual manner. The host provided a soft leather seat for me. I leaned comfortably against it during my speech, letting the words flow from me. My talk lasted three hours. Afterward, there was a Q&A session, during which I answered questions about the practice of Buddha Dharma. Unfortunately, the slanted concrete ceiling of the Ancestral Shrine had no acoustic panels installed. It produced severe echoes, rendering the quality of the recordings rather unsatisfactory. Worse, the microphone that the questioners used was not connected to the recorder, so their voices were not recorded clearly. However, this was only a minor mishap in this otherwise well-organized and well-received Dharma gathering.

The recordings of this speech were transcribed by members of the Buddhist True Enlightenment Practitioners Association. Other than smoothing out the spoken words into fluent written language, the script did not receive much polishing before going into print. In other words, what you read is pretty much what my audience heard during the actual lecture. Readers will find an abundance of colloquial expressions in this book, instead of a more elegant writing style. This was, however, a deliberate decision on my part. I wanted to faithfully present the content of my speech as well as the circumstances in which it took place so that it may one day help shed light on today's landscape of Buddhism. To benefit current and future Buddhist learners, the faithful presentation of this book is also meant to unreservedly reveal the essence of *prajñā* and the knowledge-of-the-aspects-of-paths. This preface was written before the publishing of this book to account for its background.

Xiao Pingshi
On the day of Great Heat, 2002
At the Residence of Clamor

Part III.

Foreword to *The Real and the Deluded Practitioners of Chan*

The contents of a person's actual realization of the ultimate reality must not deviate from the scriptural teachings. If a person says that "although the contents of my realization are different from the Buddhist scriptures, it is still the realization to the ultimate reality," he is without question a non-Buddhist, whether he appears a Buddhist or not. His "realization" certainly is in conflict with the true realization to the ultimate reality and is most likely a form of eternalism (*śāśvatadṛṣṭi*). This person simply fails to recognize his fallacy and therefore falsely believes his realization to be genuine.

"Scriptural teachings are derived from actual realization, while actual realization is achieved through scriptural teachings" is an axiom known to all bona fide Buddhist practitioners. This means that all genuine realizers, when decide to teach, do so based on their actual realization of the ultimate reality—for without the insights gained from actual realization, they cannot correctly delineate the profound meanings regarding the ultimate truth of the

Great Vehicle. Throughout the history, this is true for Buddha Śākyamuni from the very beginning, for all Chan patriarchs whose awakening was authentic, and for all genuine realizers of the present day. The possibility of a non-realizer to faithfully transmit the *prajñā* (wisdom about the ultimate reality) of the Great Vehicle is zero.

When an unenlightened person—one who has not truly realized the ultimate reality—attempts to propagate the *prajñā* teachings of the Great Vehicle, he inevitably takes one of the two approaches. In the first approach, he does not go beyond the literal meanings of scriptural words while honestly admits his ignorance of their profound meanings. Many prudent Buddhist teachers have chosen this route. They have never proclaimed themselves to be an enlightened noble person or misguided their students. These teachers are honorable among the unenlightened ones. However, some Buddhist teachers take the second approach. These are the ones that have reached erroneous "realization" to the ultimate reality and misunderstood the Perfection of Wisdom scriptures of the Great Vehicle, but instead of adhering to the literal meanings of the texts, they speculate on what they do not understand and deliver fallacious discourses on the principles of Chan awakening. Some do so to create an impression that they have attained high level of realization. They not only mislead their followers, but may even go as far as discrediting the true Buddha Dharma. A few typical examples include Taiwan's Buddhist masters Yin-shun (印順), Chao-hwei (昭慧), and Shing-kuang (性廣)—all of whom uphold the Prāsaṅgika Madhyamaka philosophy propagated by Tibetan tantric "Buddhism" and therefore deny the Buddha's supreme teaching of the *tathāgatagarbha*. This second approach is obviously a dishonorable way for an unenlightened person to instruct about the Buddha Dharma.

The most qualified teacher of the wondrous principles of *prajñā* is the one who crafts his instructions based on his actual realization of the ultimate reality. Consistent with the ultimate reality, the extensive and remarkable expositions delivered by such a teacher will not conflict with the true intent of the World-Honored One and the great bodhisattvas.

However, the realization to the ultimate reality is extremely difficult to attain. Throughout the history of Buddhism, genuine realizers have always been in the minority. Since the introduction of the Great Vehicle from India to China and its widespread propagation therein, seventeen hundred or so *gong'ans* of Chan awakening have been recorded, but many of which demonstrate false awakenings. Even among the few genuine realizers, the depth of their realization varies greatly, and it is not at all rare to find Chan masters who were unable to discern clearly the True Mind from the illusive mind, or only had a vague understanding of the former. Moreover, many enlightened bodhisattvas dedicate their merits for rebirths in the Pure Land of Ultimate Bliss of Buddha Amitābha, in the pure land of Bodhisattva Maitreya (i.e., the *tuṣita* heaven), or in the pure lands of other Buddhas. This means that the number of enlightened bodhisattvas returning to this world has been small, and will only continue to dwindle as time goes by.

An enlightened bodhisattva who repetitively takes rebirths into this world out of his personal vow adopts a different name or reverential title in each life. Over the course of more than a thousand years, this bodhisattva would have been known by twenty or so names. In other words, many enlightened Buddhist masters of different generations may all be the same person. This enlightened bodhisattva either did not know his previous identities due to a loss of memories across lifetimes or had deliberately withheld his previous identities until his time of departure from this world was near, so they appeared different persons. This further reduces the actual number of enlightened people. One can infer from this fact that during each era of Chinese history, genuine realizers were always in the extreme minority and it is improbable that the large number of Chan masters and monastic Buddhist masters is all enlightened. Put differently, enlightened monastics or lay Buddhists have not been and will never be the majority of any Buddhist community.

Today, there is a great number of self-proclaimed realizers in mainland China and Taiwan. Given the explanation above, it should be clear that this number cannot be true. In fact, most if not all of those self-proclaimed realizers have misidentified the "thoughtless and pristine awareness," which is but a mode of the mental consciousness, for the ultimate reality. All Buddhist disciples should be very cautious when it comes to the announcement of one's own enlightenment. False proclamation of enlightenment incurs karmic retribution in the lower destinies of rebirth, thus causing one to lose the opportunity of being human to continue Dharma cultivation. For a Buddhist disciple to descend into lower destinies under such circumstances, in spite of his sincere striving and effort, is an unfortunate irony.

While the attaining of actual realization is a feat, it is not unachievable. First of all, enlightened bodhisattvas will always be sent to this world to ensure the enduring presence of the Buddha Dharma. Second, when the guidance of a returning bodhisattva is unavailable, a practitioner can still seek enlightenment through scriptural study. The difficulty of attaining awakening to the ultimate reality in absence of the guidance of an enlightened teacher lies in the fact that most such Buddhist disciples would end up misinterpreting the meaning of scriptural texts. This has been the case for many renowned Buddhist "masters" of our time, including Yin-shun, the monastic Buddhist master of Taiwan who was given the reverential title of "venerable master (*daoshi*)." However, not every Buddhist practitioner who pursues scriptural study is subject to this pitfall. Many Chan masters of ancient times, such as Nanquan Puyuan (南泉普願), Yongjia Xuanjue (永嘉玄覺), and Yaoshan Weiyan (藥山惟儼), attained awakening on their own through scriptural study, and these self-awakened practitioners all became preeminent Chan masters of their times.

Moreover, practitioners of the Chan tradition were not the only ones who can attain actual realization of the ultimate reality through scriptural learning. Xuanzang (玄奘) and his disciple Kuiji (窺基) of the Faxiang school of Consciousness-Only, not of the Chan tradition, were both enlightened noble persons. In fact, both had reached the First Ground or beyond on the Bodhisattva Path while most of the awakened Chan masters of their time had only reached the Three Stages of Worthiness. Having entered the First Ground on the Bodhisattva Path, Xuanzang and Kuiji applied their knowledge-of-the-aspects-of-paths (*mārgakarājñatā*) to compose extensive and elaborate doctrinal exegeses that distinguish the correct teachings of the Buddha from the false views. Their doctrinal eloquence and depth of Dharma knowledge left the falsely "awakened" Chan teachers wordless whilst the genuinely awakened Chan masters read their works with admiration.

Although Bodhisattva Xuanzang was a monastic Buddhist master who propagated the teachings of the Great Vehicle, he had already mastered the *Abhidharmakośa*, a fundamental treatise of the Two Vehicles, when he encountered the Hīnayāna monk Mokṣagupta in Central Asia during his pilgrimage to India.[15] With his proficient knowledge of Hīnayāna doctrines, Xuanzang defeated Mokṣagupta in doctrinal debates, making Mokṣagupta abandon his contemptuous attitude toward him. Thereafter, Xuanzang continued his journey to India to study the Great-Vehicle treatises composed by great bodhisattvas, with which he later established the invincible doctrinal orthodoxy of the Mahāyāna Path to Buddhahood (i.e., the Bodhisattva Path) and the Hīnayāna Path to Liberation. Having benefited tremendously from his unprecedented contributions to Dharma propagation, the author of this book places Bodhisattva Xuanzang's statue with that of Buddha Śākyamuni and Bodhisattva Avalokiteśvara for veneration in the first lecture hall of the Buddhist True Enlightenment Practitioners Association to express the sincere gratitude for his endeavor.

---

[15] Due to an editorial mistake, the original Chinese text has misprinted Prajñâgupta (*bore juduo* 般若趜多) rather than Mokṣagupta as the person whom Xuanzang met in Central Asia.

In summary, the achievement of actual realization through scriptural study is neither impossible nor unheard of. But for anyone who chooses this path, the golden rule is that the contents of one's actual realization to the ultimate reality should never deviate from the doctrinal teachings expounded by the Buddha; otherwise, one's discourse and instruction will become non-Buddhist conceptualizations irrelevant to the true import of the Dharma.

Actual realization cannot depart from the correct understanding of scriptural teachings, and vice versa. Buddha Śākyamuni expounded the Path to Liberation and the Path to Buddhahood based on the perfect enlightenment he attained. He was the first person to formulate doctrinal instructions from actual realization. The oral instructions delivered by the Buddha were later committed to writing. These texts have been passed down and propagated in this world since antiquity—known as the "sūtras"—which invariably speak of the principles and contents of the ultimate reality.

When a person attains direct perception of the eighth consciousness, the mind entity that is the origin of all phenomena, by respectfully studying and reflecting on the words in the sūtras, he or she is said to have attained actual realization to the ultimate reality through scriptural study. In other words, actual realization and scriptural teachings share the same source—the ultimate reality, known as the eighth consciousness. What is awakened to is the eighth consciousness; what is taught after the awakening is the eighth consciousness. Given this inviolable principle, no Buddhist disciple should ever proclaim that the contents of his realization are at variance with the scriptural teachings. Anyone who makes this kind of statement is an ordinary being (*pṛthagjana*) bedeviled by false views. He neither understands the Buddha's teachings nor has attained authentic realization of the ultimate reality. As Chan patriarchs used to say: "To depart from the scriptures by a single word to speak as Māra the Evil One would; to interpret the scriptures literally is to do injustice to Buddhas of the past, the present, and the future."[16]

The path of cultivation of the Great Vehicle is consisted of fifty-two stages of fruition: the ten stages of Faith, the Three Stages of Worthiness, the ten Grounds, Virtual Enlightenment, Sublime Enlightenment, and the ultimate fruition of Buddhahood. Insomuch that the Chan school belongs to the Great Vehicle, a stage of fruition can certainly be assigned to the awakening attained in the Chan school. Likewise, there are clear stages of fruition in the Two Vehicles: from that of stream-entry (*srotaāpanna*), once-returning (*sakṛdāgāmin*), non-returning (*anāgāmin*), to arhat liberated through insight (*prajñāvimukta*), *arhat* doubly liberated through the power of insight and meditative absorption (*ubhayatobhāgavimukta*), great *arhat* with three knowledges (*trividyā*) and six supernatural powers (*abhijñā*), or solitary-realizer (*pratyekabuddha*). In brief, the cultivation of all Three Vehicles of the Buddha Dharma will result in ascertainable fruitions.

Some people claim that their realization of the ultimate reality does not result in the attainment of any of the fruitions within the Three Vehicles, or even that the fruition they have realized cannot

---

[16] *Jingde Era Transmission of the Lamp Record* (*Jingde chuandeng lu* 景德傳燈錄), CBETA, T51, no. 2076, 250a8-9: 問依經解義三世佛怨。離經一字。如同魔說如何。師云。固守動用三世佛怨，此外別求即同魔說。

be assessed because it is the direct attainment of Buddhahood. If the "Buddhahood" they have attained does not correspond to any one of the fifty-two stages on the Bodhisattva Path presented in Buddhist scriptures, what they have attained is unquestionably a "heterodox Buddhahood." Any level of *prajñā* a Buddhist practitioner realizes will correspond to an ascertainable fruition on the Bodhisattva Path, and a real Buddhist practitioner will always determine his or her level of attainment prudently and accurately rather than allow the judgment to be skewed by arrogance. Moreover, the incapacity to determine one's own level of attainment indicates the lack of wisdom to conduct self-assessment. When a practitioner does not even know which stage of the Bodhisattva Path he has reached, how is it possible for him to know how to advance to Buddhahood in orderly stages? He is a fool blinded by hollow and false idea, and there is no substance in his grandiose declaration of "having achieved Buddhahood immediately after awakening." A clear and proper understanding of the relationship between actual realization of the Dharma and the attainments on the Bodhisattva Path is critical to all Buddhist practitioners. It will ensure that one does not delude oneself or mislead others about one's attainment, thus bringing misfortune to one's future rebirths.

The initial realization to the eighth consciousness, the mind of true suchness, is foundational in the cultivation of the Buddha Dharma. Only when a practitioner has attained direct realization of the eighth consciousness can he or she proceed through the bodhisattva stages to eventually attain Buddhahood. More specifically, the "fundamental wisdom of non-discrimination"[17]—the "wisdom of original enlightenment"[18] of the ālaya-consciousness (the eighth consciousness) mentioned in the *Flower Garland Sūtra* (*Avataṃsaka Sūtra*) and the *Treatise on the Awakening of Faith According to the Mahāyāna*—acquired from the initial awakening to the eighth consciousness is the doorway to Buddhahood. Without realizing this foundational and sublime wisdom of the original enlightenment of the eighth consciousness, a practitioner cannot enter this doorway and will never be able to reach Buddhahood. But after one has entered this doorway, how should one attain Buddhahood through stage-by-stage cultivation? The answer: the cultivation of the knowledge-of-all-aspects.

There is no Buddha in the worlds of ten directions who has attained Buddhahood without perfectly realizing the knowledge-of-all-aspects. The great *arhats* cannot attain Buddhahood because they have not realized the *prajñā* with respect to the original enlightenment of the eighth consciousness. The great bodhisattvas have realized *prajñā* with respect to the original enlightenment of the eighth consciousness; they have not yet attained Buddhahood because they have not perfected their knowledge-of-all-aspects. In other words, the knowledge-of-all-aspects constitutes the central cultivation of Buddhahood, without which it is impossible to attain this ultimate fruition.

Sadly, not only are the contents of the knowledge-of-all-aspects no longer known by today's Buddhist disciples, some people have

---

[17] fundamental wisdom of non-discrimination: *genben wufenbie zhi* 根本無分別智.
[18] wisdom of original enlightenment: *benjue zhi* 本覺智.

even gone so far as to refute the existence of its basis, the eighth consciousness (i.e., the *tathāgatagarbha*). Despite the fact that they have not realized the eighth consciousness, the contents of the various kinds of seeds (*bīja*) it contains, or the knowledge-of-all-aspects, these people brazenly assert that the mental consciousness is the mind of the ultimate reality, that the awakening to the True Mind bears no relationship to scriptural teachings, and that the Yogācārin teaching of higher knowledge (i.e., the knowledge-of-all-aspects) is less profound than the knowledge-of-general-aspect and knowledge-of-specific-aspects pertaining to *prajñā*.[19]

In truth, the knowledge-of-all-aspects can only be cultivated after the realization of the knowledge-of-general-aspect and knowledge-of-specific-aspects pertaining to *prajñā*; yet, having neither cultivated nor realized the knowledge-of-all-aspects, these people blunderingly classify it into a lower level of wisdom than the other two. Most absurdly, they proclaim that the Yogācārin teaching of the knowledge-of-all-aspects is inferior to the idea of "the impermanent mental consciousness as the True Mind," a misconception held by unenlightened people. It is almost impossible to address a mistake this grievous.

In view of their egregious misunderstandings, our teacher Sun Cheng-de decided to analyze and refute their mistaken views with copious amounts of explanations. Her patience and earnest dedication to rectifying these misconceptions fill every page of this book. It is hoped that this work will be of benefit to all Chan

---

[19] knowledge-of-general-aspect: *zongxiang zhi* 總相智; knowledge-of-specific-aspects: *biexiang zhi* 別相智.

practitioners. Before her book went to print, Teacher Sun invited me to pen the foreword for it. May this short overview of relevant doctrinal matters provide some background of the central issues of this book for the readers.

Xiao Pingshi
Early spring of 2005

PART IV.

Excerpts from *Behind the Façade of Tibetan Tantra*

However, in all sūtras of the Three Vehicles, the Buddha professes that the Dharma-body (*dharmakāya*) of all sentient beings is the essence of the eighth consciousness that each sentient being individually and inherently possesses. The eighth consciousness itself is neither created by the seeds (*bija*) nor generated through the accumulation of the seeds. Uncreated and primordial, it perfectly *is* and has existed since beginningless time. In *The Eight Thousand Stanza Perfection of Wisdom Sūtra* and *The Twenty-Five Thousand Perfection of Wisdom Sūtra*, the Buddha uses several terms for the eighth consciousness: "the non-mind mind," "the signless mind," "the thoughtless mind," "the non-abiding mind," "the mind of bodhisattvas," and so on. In addition, the Buddha says that this Dharma-body that has existed since beginningless time it inherently possesses immeasurable pure and impure seeds. Thus, a Buddhist practitioner can rely on the pure seeds to accomplish the meritorious qualities of Buddhahood. (Vol. 1, 289)

Moreover, in all scriptures of Exoteric Buddhism, *tathāgatagarbha*—also known as the eighth consciousness or the ālaya-consciousness—is always characterized as a permanent mind entity that is with neither origination nor extinction, and is self-existing since beginningless time. This true Mind is also extensively described in the sūtras as the one that never possesses the perceptual faculties of seeing, hearing, feeling, or knowing . . . . (Vol. 1, 291-292)

Past and present gurus of Tibetan "Buddhism" often interpret the meanings of Buddhist doctrines conveniently according to their own ideas, instead of exploring and following the correct meanings. In doing so, they have muddled Buddhist doctrines into an incoherent disarray, taking themselves and their adherents far astray. In addition, tantric gurus have adulterated Buddhist cultivation with non-Buddhist practices of drops (*bindu*), energy-winds (*prāṇa*), and the like. They assign terms of Buddhist cultivation to these practices as they like and proclaim that they can bring about Buddhist enlightenment . . . .

All Buddhist learners should know that the ālaya-consciousness is not only the basis for sentient beings' interminable transmigration within the three realms, but also the basis for every noble person's realization of nirvana. An arhat of the fixed Hearer-Vehicle (*śrāvakayāna*) disposition, who does not convert to the Great Vehicle, will extinguish every one of the eighteen elements at the end of his life, after eliminating the self-view (*ātmadṛṣṭi*) and self-attachment (*ātmagraha*) as a result of cultivating the Path to Liberation. Since his mental faculty (*manas*, one of the eighteen elements)[20] will not reappear, the eighth consciousness, perpetually non-evaluating, undiscerning, and non-controlling, will not bring about further rebirths in the three realms and is therefore designated as the "nirvana without remainder." Without the regeneration of the mental faculty, there will be no mind entity to direct the eighth consciousness to enter an embryo and give rise to further rebirths.

When an *arhat* enters the nirvana without remainder by eliminating the eighteen elements, all that remains is the eighth consciousness. Neither the consciousnesses with the perceptual faculties of hearing, seeing, feeling, and knowing, nor contact with the six sense-objects will reappear in the nirvana without remainder. Thus, the nirvana without remainder is characterized as "tranquil and quiescent." In addition to "tranquil and quiescent," the nirvana without remainder is also described as apart from the "impermanence of all compounded phenomena," because the mental activities of the seven evolving consciousnesses—the

---

[20] The mental faculty, *manendriya* or *manas* in Sanskrit and *yigen* 意根 in Chinese, is one of the six sense faculties (*indriya*), but unlike the first five sense faculties, it is a mental entity unassociated with a physical organ. The sense faculties and their corresponding sense objects are essential conditions for the arising of the first six consciousnesses (*vijñāna*); the *manas* is called the mental faculty as it is required for the arising of the mental consciousness (*manovijñāna*). It should be noted that in addition to being a sense faculty, the mental faculty is also one of the eight forms of consciousness in the Yogācāra's teaching of eight consciousnesses, in which it is known as the afflicted mental consciousness (*kliṣṭamanas*; *mona shi* 末那識).

evaluating and willing activities of the mental faculty and the perceiving activities of the first six consciousnesses—are all nonexistent.

Furthermore, the nirvana without remainder is also said to be real and without a self. The eighth consciousness itself does not possess the perceptual faculties and the evaluating and willing properties of the first seven consciousnesses. Since these properties of the first seven consciousnesses have already been thoroughly extinguished when an *arhat* enters the nirvana without remainder, the self can neither exist nor manifest in the nirvana with remainder. For this reason, the nirvana without remainder is not in the non-Buddhist concept of "selfhood" that are invalidated by the Dharma Seal "all phenomena are without a self." A true nirvana without remainder must conform to these Three Dharma Seals.

From the previous explanation, one can see that the eighth consciousness, or the ālaya-consciousness, is the basis for the cultivation and realization of nirvana. It is the essence of nirvana. Without it, there would be no nirvana to realize and nirvana would be a state of nihilistic nothingness. (Vol. 1, 293-294)

Most lama gurus regard the "emptiness of all phenomena," rather than the eighth consciousness, as the Dharma-body....

... [A]ccording to Tibetan "Buddhism," the "emptiness of all phenomena" refers to the existence of the conscious mind alone, together with the drop (*bindu*), while one is not visualizing or allowing any phenomenon to arise. Tibetan "Buddhism" defines the Dharma-body as this mental state of the "emptiness of all phenomena." Furthermore, the generation of all other phenomena through visualization of the drop is theorized in Tibetan "Buddhism" as the first six consciousnesses' function of phenomenal manifestation, which they define as the "emanation body." If, while abiding in the state of the drop, the conscious mind retains its "luminous nature" (awareness) without any taints and attachment, this luminosity of the conscious mind is defined is defined as the "reward body." . . . .

. . . [T]hese definitions are at odds with the teachings of the Three Vehicles and also contradict the intended meaning of Nāgārjuna's many discourses. Some tantric "patriarchs" misconstrued the Dharma-body as the drop visualized by the conscious mind, while in reality the existence of this visualized drop is contingent on the existence of the conscious mind. In other words, the Dharma-body in Tibetan "Buddhism" is but a mental state visualized by the conscious mind. Their definition of the "Dharma-body of all phenomena being emptiness" simply refers to the conscious mind's direct perception of the drop without the arising of discrimination, craving, aversion, or ignorance, and so forth. In other words, they mistake the conscious mind for the Dharma-body and declare that the conscious mind possesses luminosity—the ability to discern while abiding in a thoughtless state.

In reality, the conscious mind is a collective term for the first six consciousnesses. Being dependently originated phenomena themselves, these six consciousnesses are unable to manifest phenomenal states and are not the emanation-body. That which is discerned by the first six consciousnesses is actually the "internal image portion"[21] manifested by the eighth consciousness. (Vol. 1, 294-296)

———————————◆———————————

Even if a person can maintain the conscious mind in a thoughtless mental state for an entire day or an entire life without being drowsy or asleep, the essential nature of the conscious mind still cannot be altered. In fact, even if a person could abide in such a mental state for three or five eons, it still cannot be changed. The conscious mind will always be the conscious mind. Even when a person has reached the ultimate Buddha Ground, the conscious mind still cannot be transformed into the true suchness of Buddha Ground—also called the immaculate consciousness (*amalavijñāna*). The attempt of Tibetan "Buddhism" to transform the conscious mind into the true suchness of Buddha Ground by holding it in a thoughtless state over long periods of time is but a delusion—definitely not the correct way to practice the Buddha Dharma. After three immeasurable eons of Dharma cultivation, Buddhist practitioners could attain Buddhahood, while the

---

[21] As a seed (*bīja*) from the eighth storehouse consciousness (ālaya-consciousness) fructifies, it simultaneously produces both a moment of consciousness (*vijñāna*) and a corresponding sensory object (*ālambana*). The object, which is in fact not external to the mind, is called the "image portion" (*nimittabhāga*) or the "grasped" (*grāhya*). The perception of that object is called the "perceiving portion" (*darśanabhāga*) or the "grasper" (*grāhaka*). The awareness that perception has occurred is called the "self-witnessing portion" (*svasaṃvittibhāga*). [Robert E. Buswell and Donald S. Lopes, *The Princeton Dictionary of Buddhism*, Princeton, NJ: Princeton University Press, 2013, 108.]

tantric practitioners who refuse to return to the correct practice of the Buddha Dharma would still remain unenlightened beings, with the delusion of having attained Buddhahood. All the efforts they put into their practice over the same three immeasurable eons will end up fruitless. (Vol. 1, 299-300)

Part V.

Excerpts from *The Essence of Buddhist Enlightenment: The Awakened Eye*

For a practitioner to achieve "awakening to the Way," nothing is faster than Chan; for a teacher to bring about awakened students, nothing is more effective than Chan. [In this Dharma-ending era,] it is extremely unlikely to find a person who has achieved authentic awakening within the traditions of tantric "Buddhism" in Japan and Tibet—this is not only the case in ancient times, but is still so in the modern age. (177)

The cultivation of the Great Vehicle is down to earth, solid, and tangible. It follows a step-by-step course. Every stage is verifiable with the sūtras and treatises. It is fundamentally different from Tibetan "Buddhism," which does not employ real cultivation or achieve true realizations, but uses the occult manifestation of ghosts and spirits and the self-promotional words of unenlightened tantric patriarchs to justify their false claims of attainments. (211)

Buddhist practitioners who want to swiftly attain Buddhahood should first seek to reach the Path of Vision on the Mahāyāna Bodhisattva Path by attaining awakening to the True Mind via Chan contemplation. One should not follow Tibetan "Buddhism" to engage in cultivation that will never lead to the realization of the True Mind. More important, one should not take up the sexual practices of Highest Yoga Tantra, which is a practice of Hindu origin that induces connection with evil spirits and bestial demons (yakṣas). Falling victim to financial or sex scams is not the worst outcome; breaking Buddhist precepts and undermining the Buddha Dharma will result in far more severe consequences. Every practitioner should treat this matter with caution. Chan offers the speediest way to arrive at the Path of Vision of the Mahāyāna Bodhisattva Path—by awakening to the True Mind in one sudden thought, one enters the stage of being "a Buddha in semblance."[22] Those with sufficient stock of merits and roots of virtue could even make it to the First Ground in a single lifetime. (211)

---

[22] The Chinese Tiantai school proposed the teaching of the Sixfold Identification with Buddha (liuji fo 六即佛) based on the Mahāyāna notion that all sentient beings possess Buddha-nature and are inherently Buddha. It set forth six progressive stages that an ordinary being goes through to attain the perfect enlightenment of Buddha: 1. Buddha in principle, 2. Buddha in name, 3. Buddha in contemplation, 4. Buddha in semblance, 5. Buddha in progressive realization, and 6. Buddha in ultimate Buddhahood. A person who has awakened to the True Mind in the Chan tradition is said to have reached the stage of "Buddha in semblance" because he or she has attained direct comprehension of the essence of Buddha. "Buddha in semblance" also corresponds to the Path of Vision in the Yogācāra classification of the bodhisattva stages.

Ignorance (*avidyā*) means foolishness and benightedness. In the Buddha Dharma, ignorance refers to sentient beings' nescience of the ultimate reality (i.e., Emptiness).[23] This is why, in the sūtras of the Great Vehicle, sentient beings who are bound by cyclical existence within the three realms are called "ordinary beings," while the hearers and solitary-realizers of the Two Vehicles, albeit attaining fruitions and therefore venerated as "noble," are still called "the fools." As the noble persons of the Two Vehicles cannot realize the ultimate reality, they and the ordinary beings of the three realms are referred together as "the ordinary beings and the fools." In other words, any individual who cannot understand, who misunderstands, or who is doubtful of the ultimate reality is said to be a fool. Therefore, despite their having already attained liberation from the three realms, the adepts (*aśaikṣa*) who have completed the training of the Two Vehicles are called fools all the same. (274)

---

[23] The eighth consciousness (i.e., the *tathāgatagarbha*) exhibits the thoroughly established nature (*pariniṣpanna-svabhāva*), also called the nature of suchness (*tathatā*); "thoroughly established" and "suchness" describe its being a real existence as well as its imperturbability by all phenomenal objects. Insomuch that the essence of the eighth consciousness is empty of the imagined nature (*parikalpita-svabhāva*) and the other-dependent nature (*paratantra-svabhāva*), it is called Emptiness (*śūnyatā; kongxing* 空性). In Buddhist literature, "Emptiness" and "the mind of true suchness" are often used as synonyms to the eighth consciousness and the *tathāgatagarbha*. The word "Emptiness" is capitalized here to differentiate it from the emptiness that characterizes the absence of any intrinsic existence (*svabhāva*).

The awakening to the True Mind cannot be attained through observing the conscious mind. A person who has not awakened to the True Mind does not know where it is, so how can he observe it? Awakening cannot be attained by observing the conscious mind, but has to be attained by searching for the True Mind. That said, before one sets out searching for the True Mind, he should understand that the "thoughtless pristine awareness" is an unreal and illusory phenomenon. He should look for a mind that exists in concurrence with this thoughtless awareness, but is itself without any awareness of the sense-objects. In other words, he should contemplate Chan by searching for the True Mind rather than contemplating the illusory mind, whereby he looks for the True Mind that has, since beginningless time, never exhibited the awareness associated with the three realms. The best method to search for the True Mind is none other than the contemplation of *huatou* and *gong'an* (36).

Chan master Xinghua Cunjiang (興化存獎) was the teacher of Emperor Zhuangzong of the Later Tang (唐莊宗). One day, Emperor Zhuangzong said to his teacher, "I acquired a priceless pearl when I conquered Daliang, but nobody has offered a price for it." "Your majesty, please let me have a look at the pearl." The emperor untied his scarf with his hands [to show the pearl]. The master said, "A treasure of an emperor, who dares to offer a price for it?" Chan master Xuanjue (玄覺) heard this *gong'an* and asked the elders from various regions, "Please comment on this, all of you. Does the reply of Chan master Xinghua confirm Zhuangzong's awakening? Or does it reject it? If it confirms his awakening, may I ask where does Xinghua's Dharma-eye lie? If it rejects his awakening, what is the fault of Emperor Zhuangzong?"[24]

More than a thousand years later, the author shall take the liberty to answer Zhuangzong's question for Xinghua: "It is worth exactly everything under Heaven!" Do my words affirm Zhuangzong's awakening or not? If they don't, why do I say it is worth exactly everything under Heaven? What do I really mean? (183)

Thrangu Rinpoche (創古仁波切) said, "The conscious mind must have existed before fertilization took place in the uterus; therefore, there must be a previous life before this one. Take the fact that we have awareness and consciousness as of today. Does it mean that tomorrow our mind will cease to exist and we will have no mind? No, that is not the case. Regardless of whether the link between body and mind has broken or not, the continuity of the conscious mind would persist. Based on this logic, we can be certain of the existence of future lives, [since] there is no phenomenon that can terminate the conscious mind's continual existence. This is the teaching of the Buddha and is accepted by various Buddhist schools."

---

[24] This *gong'an* is taken from the *Jingde Era Transmission of the Lamp Record* (*Jingde chuandeng lu* 景德傳燈錄), CBETA, T51, no. 2076, 295b17-21: 師後為後唐莊宗師。莊宗一日謂。師曰。朕收大梁得一顆無價明珠。未有人酬價。師曰。請陛下珠看。帝以手舒開幞頭。師曰。君王之寶誰敢酬價（玄覺徵云。且道興化肯同光不肯同光。若肯同光興化眼在什麼處）。

The author's response: the above teaching of Thrangu Rinpoche is the exact opposite of that set forth by the Buddha, and is rejected by most Buddhist traditions except for the Prāsaṅgika Madhyamaka. That which has awareness (the conscious mind) vanishes and ceases on a daily basis. To remember yesterday's happenings, today's conscious mind must rely on the immediate antecedent condition (*samanantarapratyaya*)—the conscious mind of a preceding moment—to reconnect with yesterday's conscious mind. The conscious mind that comes into existence after one wakes up from sleep is constantly changing: arising and perishing in every moment. Its origination and extinction are analogous to the way one frame of a film gives way to the subsequent frame. Before the seed of the consciousness of the previous moment has ceased, it will relinquish its position so that the seed of the conscoiusness of the subsequent moment can manifest in its place. This continual, uninterrupted process of arising, perishing, and replacement is what makes possible the conscious mind's luminosity and awareness. The conscious mind's luminosity and awareness is in the constant flux of momentary arising and perishing, and they will instantly cease to exist the moment the conscious mind itself ceases.

The conscious mind's origination depends upon three co-existing supportive bases: the mental faculty, the ālaya-consciousness, and the five internal sense bases (i.e., the brain, which is not a self-existing phenomenon). This is what the Buddha taught and what is accepted by all Buddhist traditions. Insofar as the origination of consciousness requires the presence of these three co-existing supportive bases, the conscious mind cannot arise when the mental faculty does not will its arising. For instance, the conscious mind cannot arise and function when a person enters the two kinds of mindless absorption[25] or is in a state of dreamless sleep, during which he or she is completely unconscious. Moreover, if there is no ālaya-consciousness to collect and store the seeds of the conscious mind, the conscious mind will not arise even if the mental faculty wills it to. If a person (the mental faculty) wishing to obtain water from a tap (water being equivalent to the manifestation of the conscious mind), but no water is stored in the tank (suppose the ālaya-consciousness did not hold any seeds of the conscious mind), the person (or mental faculty) would fail to obtain any water at all. The water that has already flowed out from the tap cannot magically create more water in the tank; likewise, the consciousness of one moment cannot generate the consciousness of the next moment. It is the seeds of the conscious mind stored in the ālaya-consciousness that generates the consciousness in a seemingly continuous flow, one arising in the stead of another. This is what enables the conscious mind's function of awareness and discernment. Bodhisattva Maitreya, the author of the *Five Treatises of Maitreya* endorsed by Tibetan "Buddhism," explicates the above truth with respect to the conscious mind's origination in the *Treatise on the Stages of Yogic Practice* (*Yogācārabhūmiśāstra*) in great detail. Has Thrangu Rinpoche never heard of or read about Bodhisattva Maitreya's discourse? Or has he read it but failed to comprehend its

---

[25] The two mindless absorptions refer to the "meditative absorption of nonperception (*asaṃjñāsamāpatti*)" and "meditative absorption of cessation (*nirodhasamāpatti*)."

meaning? At any rate, how could he claim that the consciousness of the previous moment can generate the consciousness of the next moment?

Furthermore, the conscious mind's arising is contingent on the five internal sense bases. If the five internal sense-organs (*indriya*) are damaged or completely gone, such as in the case of brain death, the conscious mind cannot come into being and will cease forever, and so will its luminous awareness. During general anesthesia, for instance, the conscious mind ceases because the five internal sense-organs cannot function. Bearing the honorific title of "the precious one,"[26] why is the Rinpoche ignorant of these widely known facts?

Secondly, Thrangu Rinpoche believes that the conscious mind already exists before fertilization takes place in the uterus and that the consciousness of the current life continues from the previous one. His views contradict the teachings of both the Buddha and bodhisattvas. If what he said were true, every person should possess recompense-derived supernatural knowledge of past lives and would be able to access past life memories without the need to cultivate this ability. Additionally, if the consciousness of previous life never ceases, it would be able to enter, dwell in, and exit the womb, and every person would have clear awareness of these events. If that were true, Thrangu Rinpoche should be able to recall how the consciousness from his previous life entered his mother's womb, what he experienced while staying in his mother's womb (during which his mental state would have alternated be-

---

[26] The word "rinpoche" means "the precious one" in Tibetan.

tween sleep and awareness), and the process of his own birth. But Thrangu Rinpoche, as well as anyone without supernatural power to remember one's former lives, has no recollection of any of these events.

This is clear evidence that the conscious mind does not exist when the eighth consciousness first enters the womb. Its arising depends upon the existence of the five sense bases of the current life, the mental faculty, and the eighth consciousness. The absence of any one of these three contingent factors results in the cessation of the conscious mind. As the physical brain of the current life (i.e., the five internal sense-bases) slowly develops to full maturity, the conscious mind goes from nonexistent to indistinct to manifest. If the five sense-bases perish, the conscious mind of the current life would cease forever along with them; it cannot move on to the next life. It is the ālaya-consciousness, which collects and stores the seeds of the conscious mind of the current life as well as all karmic seeds, that takes rebirth following the will of the mental faculty and in accordance with either the individual's karma or wish.

Expounded by the Buddha, this truth is stated clearly in the scriptures and treatises, and is recognized by all schools of the Great Vehicle. However, adherents of Prāsaṅgika Madhyamaka adopt Tsongkhapa's erroneous views and reject the existence of both the mental faculty and the ālaya-consciousness. They cling to the notion that the consciousness is without origination and cessation, can transmigrate to future lives, and is the contingent basis of all phenomena (for details, please refer to Tsongkhapa's *Illumination of the Thought: An Extensive Explanation of Chandrakirti's "Supplement to* the 'Middle Way'"[27] and *Essence of Eloquence on the Provisional and Definitive*).[28] This view is inconsistent with the teachings of Buddha Śākyamuni and Bodhisattva Maitreya as it denies the ultimate foundation of the Buddha Dharma. On what grounds can any school that preaches the Prāsaṅgika Madhyamaka regard itself as Buddhist?

If the conscious mind were indeed without origination and cessation, it could not possess awareness and discernment. The reasoning for this truth is discoursed in great length in my book *The Undeniable Existence of the Tathāgatagarbha*.[29] Furthermore, if the conscious mind were not to cease ever, it would be continuously aware and discerning, but the Buddha taught that it does cease to exist in the "five mindless states": dreamless sleep, syncope, the absorption of non-perception, the absorption of cessation, and thorough death. If the conscious mind never ceases or terminates, as Thrangu Rinpoche claims, its discerning function should manifest without interruption at all times. If that were the case, a person would be aware of being in the five mindless states—and these five mindless states should never have existed in the first place. Thrangu Rinpoche's teaching not only contradicts the Buddha's teachings, but also goes against observable reality. How could the Rinpoche liberate sentient beings with such an absurd view? He is not teaching but misleading people.

---

27   *dbu ma dgongs pa rab gsal*; *ru zhonglun shanxian miyi shu* 入中論善顯密意疏.
28   *drang nges legs bshad snying po*; *bian liao buliao yi shanshuo zanglun* 辨了不了義善說藏論.
29   Xiao Pingshi, *The Undeniable Existence of the Tathāgatagarbha* (*Zhenshi rulai zang* 真實如來藏), Taipei: True Wisdom Publishing Co., 2000.

If Thrangu Rinpoche wants to rid himself of these false views and understand the absurdity of the teachings transmitted by the gurus of Prāsaṅgika Madhyamaka as well as the four major sects of Tibetan "Buddhism" he has to realize for himself the *tathāgatagarbha*—the Emptiness. To this end, I shall draw the Rinpoche's attention to the public case of Chan master Baiyun and the shoe bag:

> One day, Master Baiyun Shixing (白雲實性) of Shaozhou declared to the assembly, "Do you all understand Emptiness? All you have to do is to experience it along streets and lanes where pigs are slaughtered and meat is chopped up in that boiling soup of hell. Only a person who has comprehended it personally in this way can teach and sculpt another. Such a person is a world apart from one who learns it from the monks in the monasteries. There is yet another type who only sits on the long bench in the Chan hall meditating and dares not to do anything bad. So you tell me: which of these two kinds of persons has more advantage? If nobody has anything to say, go take a rest!"[30]

---

[30] This *gong'an* is taken from the *Jingde Era Transmission of the Lamp Record* (*Jingde chuandeng lu* 景德傳燈錄), CBETA, T51, no. 2076, 384c9-13: 師上堂謂眾曰。諸人會麼。但街頭市尾屠兒魁膾地獄鑊湯處會取。若恁麼會堪與人為師為匠。若向衲僧門下天地懸殊。更有一般底。只向長連床上作好人去。汝道此兩般人那箇有長處。無事珍重。

Chan master Baiyun asked a monk, "From where did you come?" The monk answered, "From Yunmen." Baiyun asked again, "How many heads of water buffalo are there in Yunmen [i.e. how many people have achieved awakening]?" The monk replied, "One or two." Chan master Baiyun commended, "Good water buffaloes." After giving his praise, he asked again, "How would you describe the true suchness and the ultimate reality without giving up the false appearances and the words and letters of the mundane world?" The monk answered, "This is a chair." Chan master Baiyun pushed the monk, and said, "Go get me my shoe bag!" The monk was at a loss for what to do. Later on, upon learning this public case, Chan master Yunmen immediately remarked, "Only Chan master Baiyun could have done this!"[31]

Whether past or present, many prominent practice centers teach monastics to contemplate Chan by means of sitting meditation; this is how they impart the Dharma to disciples. So for what reason did Chan master Baiyun advise against such a practice? And why instead did he tell his monastic disciples to go figure it out along the streets where pigs and lambs are slaughtered? Those are places of extreme cruelty, hells for animals in

---

[31] Ibid., CBETA, T51, no. 2076, 384c13-18: 師問僧。什麼處來。曰雲門來。師曰。裏許有多少水牛。曰一箇兩箇。師曰。好水牛。師問僧。不壞假名而譚實相作麼生。僧曰。遮箇是椅子。師以手撥云。將鞋袋來。僧無對（雲門和尚聞之乃云。須是他始得）。

this world, where they are chopped up with hatchets and knives and tossed into cauldrons of boiling soup. What is there to figure out? Why did Baiyun tell monks who always stay far away from pungent herbs and meat to seek answers in places that reek of such nauseating stench? I too would persuade Thrangu Rinpoche to figure out the true suchness (i.e., Emptiness) in such foul places. Do not close your eyes to visualize a sky-traveller (*ḍākinī*), a meditational deity (*yidam*), or any such objects; for these visualizations are objects of the deluded mind, and the kind of Chan practiced by an unenlightened person. Irrelevant to the ultimate truth, these visualizations will not result in awakening even after eons.

If Thrangu Rinpoche is willing to figure out what Chan is in places where pigs and lambs are slaughtered in Tibet, he may catch a glimpse of the *tathāgatagarbha* (i.e., Emptiness). After that, he can always see that this mind of Emptiness dwells amid the aggregates, sense-fields, and elements of a sentient being; never will he lose this insight, unless he denies it due to insufficient faith and wisdom. Once the Rinpoche has spotted the mind of Emptiness, he would be able to examine and pinpoint the erroneous and absurd notions transmitted by the four main sects of Tibetan "Buddhism." With this knowledge, he should approach all well-established practice centers of Tibetan "Buddhism" worldwide and tell their followers to return to their hometowns in Tibet and India to watch the slaying of cows and lambs in the streets! Then, every adherent of Tibetan "Buddhism" would become a son of the "lion king" (i.e., Buddha) who can roar the lion's roar—illuminating the Buddha Dharma by destroying misconceptions. Tibetan

"Buddhism" would be transformed from the core and the Buddha Dharma would flourish and bloom.

One day, Chan master Baiyun asked a monk, "Where do you come from?" The monk replied, "From Yunmen." A quick and clever one would have gotten the point before answering the question and would have prostrated to Baiyun right away. Baiyun was kind, though. He did not give the monk a beating, but waited for a more opportune occasion to ask him, "How many awakened people are there at Yunmen?" The monk replied, "One or two." Baiyun said, "Good water buffaloes." This pointer was hard to get. Seeing that the monk was slow to pick up his clues, Baiyun threw himself in and asked in plain words, "How would you describe the true suchness and the ultimate reality without giving up the imputed language of the mundane world?" The monk had learned some superficial tricks from various places, so he tried his luck with them and said, "This is a chair." If I were there, I would have taken the chair and threw it out of the door, and said, "This is not a chair!" This is called "chipping and pecking simultaneously" in Chan. But Baiyun took a most unexpected approach. He pushed the monk and said, "Bring me my shoe bag!" If the monk was one with adequate merits and wisdom, he could have figured it out right when he fetched and handed in Baiyun's shoe bag. Unfortunately, he did not know what to do. If I were there, I would have bellowed, "You don't even know how to fetch a shoe bag!" But that monk's plumage was not full yet, so Baiyun left him alone. Chan master Yunmen later heard about this public case and sighed, "Only Chan master Baiyun could have done it this way!" One can take from Yunmen's comment that there were a lot of "wild foxes" among Chan masters of his day. What he meant was that the various Buddhist masters could not understand Baiyun's snake-toying tricks.

Thrangu Rinpoche journeyed thousands of miles from northern India to Taiwan. Known as "an island of treasures", Taiwan certainly has the great treasure of the supreme Dharma. If the Rinpoche doesn't want to be ridiculed, he should by all means not leave this island of treasure empty-handed, but scour this island for the Dharma treasure. If he cannot find it, he should come see me. Request a meeting with me at the Buddhist True Enlightenment Practitioners Association. When I see the Rinpoche at the door, I will call out, "Rinpoche!" If he has not understood what I mean when he responds to my greeting, I would say, "Take off your leather shoes and go inside!" If the Rinpoche still does not get it after he has entered the building, of what use is all that he knows? (313-318)

《平實導師法語選輯》

編輯序言

　　經過兩千五百多年的流傳,佛教由一個局限在印度部分地區的地域性宗教發展成普及世界的全球性宗教。雖然今日佛教已有全球性的知名度與影響力,但由於佛法宗旨甚深難解,佛教日趨世俗化,而實證佛法的修行方法,也同時被嚴重扭曲而偏離了 佛陀的教導。修行佛法的究竟目的,難道只是當前佛教所強調的行善積德、屏除貪欲、潛心正念,與追求心靈的平靜與世俗快樂而已?平實導師對佛法深入淺出的系統性演述,彰顯出 佛陀的教導雖然包含世俗利益上的修行,然而其核心義理是要實證「真心」,也就是宇宙萬物的「根本因」。釋迦牟尼佛正是因為具足一切世間和超越世間的智慧與能力,才能被冠以「正遍知」、「世間解」和「人天導師」等十個尊貴稱號。

　　除了世俗化之外,現代佛教逐漸脫離實證本質而成為單純的學術研究項目。針對此現象,平實導師自出世弘法以來,一向強調佛法必須實修實證。而實修實證的基礎是對教義的正確認知以及遵循佛陀所軌範的修證內涵與次第。為了讓佛弟子能夠通過真修實證獲得可以實際應用在生活中的佛法智慧,乃至了悟生命實相,平實導師融合完整的佛法教理與修證行門,編製了三個層次分明的佛學課程。

初級與中級課程包括建立正確的佛法知見，六度波羅蜜的修學，以及教導學人極具成效的動中修定法門，以幫助佛弟子能夠進一步參禪證悟。在高級課程中，平實導師更為已經證悟的菩薩弟子們，教授入地前應修習之般若智慧乃至初地菩薩以上應修學的深妙佛法。

以要言之，佛法的修證必須建立在正確理解佛陀所說的教法與實證的體驗之上。實證與純粹理論上的理解有別，實證必然奠基於法義上的正確理解，但無實證而只是純粹理論上的理解則常導致錯誤的結論。為了讓學人能夠正確以及深入瞭解佛陀的聖教，平實導師詳細註解了三乘佛法中多部重要經論，包括《楞伽經詳解》、《心經密意》、《阿含正義》、《楞嚴經講記》、《金剛經宗通》、《維摩詰經講記》、《優婆塞戒經講記》等。除了這些講解佛經要義的作品，他對佛法修證內涵的論述，如《無相念佛》、《念佛三昧修學次第》、《真假開悟》、《禪淨圓融》、《公案拈提》七輯、《真實如來藏》、《狂密與真密》四輯等著作，也受到讀者廣大的迴響。

平實導師對佛法教義的精妙解釋與修證指導，促使學佛人和佛教學者重新檢視他們對佛法本質的理解和認知，在佛教界引起極大迴響。不同於當今一般大師的照本宣科，平實導師深入闡釋佛法三乘經律論的真實義理，在其著作中將完整的佛法修證次第與內涵，以及長期以來普遍困擾修行人和學者的疑難及議題，提供了簡單明確、條分縷析的論述和清楚透徹的說明。這些議題包括：

❖ 《阿含經》中，對於眾生生死之間因果業種的傳遞，以及小乘聲聞與緣覺解脫道的修證，是否皆肯定需要有一個常住心體的存在？

- ❖ 貫通三乘佛法體系的核心義理為何?
- ❖ 第二轉法輪與第三轉法輪教義,何者層次較高而為究竟了義說?
- ❖ 釋迦牟尼佛所教導的究竟是六識論還是八識論?
- ❖ 釋迦牟尼佛是否否定現象界一切萬物背後有一永恆存在的本體?
- ❖ 看話頭和參究公案是禪宗幫助修行人破參明心的方便法門,究竟學人應該如何具足看話頭和參公案所需要的禪定功夫?
- ❖ 禪宗的開悟是真實而可親證的嗎?
- ❖ 開悟的本質與所證之標的為何?開悟之後的修學次第與內涵為何?
- ❖ 意識心能夠達到「一念不生」的境界就是開悟嗎?
- ❖ 藏傳喇嘛教之教義符合三乘佛法教義嗎?

依於佛陀所說三乘諸經教理與親證的實修體驗,平實導師主張:

- ❖ 一切佛法不是抽象概念的理論,而是真實可證的真理。
- ❖ 三乘諸經淺深次第的教理皆是依法界實相——真心如來藏而建立。《阿含經》中所說的入胎識和十因緣教義,即是第八識如來藏真實存在的隱覆開示。依此含藏無量功能與業種的如來藏,一切眾生造業受報與轉世於六道輪迴的現象得以成就。
- ❖ 確定佛法為八識論:前五個感官識、第六識意識、第七識末那識,與第八識阿賴耶識(根本識)。一切三界世間現象與出世間的涅槃解脫,皆依此八識而能成就。《華嚴經》說：「三界唯心、萬法唯識」，這個境界確實是可以實證的及檢驗。

❖ 禪宗開悟所證之真心，正是經教中所說的如來藏、阿賴耶識、第八識、真如、無心相心以及空性。而如來藏的體性真實存在，即是大乘經中所說「空」義的所依本體，確實可證，並非只是一想像觀念或施設名相。

❖ 於三轉法輪教義中，第三轉之唯識、如來藏經教所說有關一切種智的修習，是最了義究竟的佛法。

❖ 佛弟子實證如來藏、發起般若智慧之前，必須完成相當的布施、持戒、忍辱、精進、禪定、與聞熏般若知見六度的修行。

❖ 開悟親證如來藏，是一切佛弟子於佛道修行中最重要與必經的階位。開悟之後必須於如來藏境界能夠安忍不退，才是真正進入佛菩提道的見道位中。親證如來藏後，只是進入佛道修證位階之第七住位，尚有無量法門必須修學方能成就圓滿佛果。

❖ 所有大乘佛法與小乘佛法的果證，都必須有相應的定力作為基礎。

❖ 喇嘛教所說無上瑜伽雙身修法，其所證未超越八識中的意識或前六識境界，尚未企及佛教所說的如來藏境界；其中所說的生起次第與圓滿次第法義本質，違背三乘佛法的修證教理，而且背道而馳。

❖ 月稱、宗喀巴，與當代許多法師，譬如印順等，所信受的應成派中觀思想，本質上是萬法緣起性空的無因唯緣論，違背於 佛陀所說有一真實常住的如來藏為緣起根本因之法教。

編輯者從平實導師百多本著作中,挑選出與學佛人最有切身關係的精要內容引介給讀者。本書內容分為五部分:

(一) 《無相念佛》序言:平實導師的第一本著作《無相念佛》,乃是《楞嚴經》中所說大勢至菩薩念佛圓通法門的入門修行方法。在此序言裡,著者簡要述說其自身如何經由修學此方便法門而得證悟實相的過程。

(二) 《大乘無我觀》序言:在此序言裡,著者簡要述說在整個佛道的修證過程裡,開悟證得如來藏、發起般若智慧,與修證趣近一切種智之間的種種關係內涵。

(三) 《真假禪和》序言:著者概說佛弟子所證得之宗門意旨(第八識如來藏),不能違背於佛陀所說佛法教理。佛弟子證得真心,現觀其真如無分別性,才能進一步修學圓滿佛地所必須成就的一切種智。

(四) 《狂密與真密》選錄:喇嘛教之坦特羅教理和修行方法,即使連小乘佛法解脫道的初果也不能證得,何況明心開悟、證得博大精深的大乘佛法。事實上,喇嘛教的修行方法,不但不能幫助修行人解脫三界輪迴,只更加重修行人的我見與我執。其觀想本尊之行門與男女雙身法,全部落在意識等五蘊境界中,并非真心本來無分別之境界。喇嘛教的修學與果證,根本與三乘佛法無關。

(五) 《宗門道眼》選錄：佛道的圓滿，必須經過三大無量數劫的次第修行，才能成就。在這過程中，證悟真心是最關鍵與根本的突破。所證的真心，即是如來藏，是本質為空性的心，不是一般人所認識的意識心；意識心永遠有分別的體性，不論於任何修證境界，都不可能轉變成本來即無分別的真心。只有實證真心的佛弟子，才能真正看懂禪宗公案的涵義。

　　本書所選編的內容，雖然只是平實導師著作中極小部分，然而其中所顯示清晰與深刻的佛法內涵，在當今之絕大多數佛教著作中難得一見。不論您是佛弟子、學者、還是有興趣瞭解佛教的讀者，本書對於佛法真實意義的說明，都能為您提供前所未見的明確觀點與令人發起洞見智慧的認知。

一・《無相念佛》自序

對一般佛弟子而言,所謂念佛,係指稱念佛菩薩聖號。因虔誠地不斷唱念或默念,至心信賴歸向,而獲得佛菩薩之冥感或顯相之感應。其普遍而主要的目的在求將來捨此報身時,得蒙佛菩薩接引往生極樂淨土。而十方諸佛淨土,包括 本師釋迦世尊的淨土,其實無量無數,不可稱計,非僅阿彌陀佛的極樂國土而已。此外,淨土亦有唯心淨土與諸佛化土之別。

若廣義而言,大乘佛教之一切教法莫非念佛法門,莫非淨土法門。包括眾所周知的:持佛名號、持咒、禮佛、供養、止觀、持戒、課誦、抄經、閱讀、解說、憶念、思惟、參究……等等,其目的皆在學佛之行,入佛知見,證佛解脫,得佛功德,乃至成佛,成就四種淨土,是為廣義的念佛。

禪與淨土其實密不可分。欲得成佛,非僅持念佛名可辦,必賴禪定悟明心性。見道之後,速得晉入修道之位,佛果可期。然欲見道,需賴參禪或止觀法門之理觀,此則非定力莫辦,尤其是動中的工夫。而念佛人欲持名念佛至一心不亂,亦需工夫。若能以持名念佛及禮佛為方便,欲入大勢至菩薩念佛圓通法門,並非難事;則往生極樂淨土便有把握。亦可參究念佛：所謂「不假方便，自得心開」，非無可能。若以念佛圓通法門之初步工夫轉而參禪，則無門之門自然現前，欲得悟明心性，亦有希望。即知禪與淨土，密不可分。

佛弟子若能以「禪定心要」修行淨土法門，以淨土法門之助益成就動中工夫，則無論修學禪或淨土，皆能得力，速獲成績。末學不揣譾陋，提出以上看法，欲以淺薄之經驗，粗鄙之文筆，效野人之獻曝。但求利益眾生，不計個人毀譽，執筆為文，漸積篇幅，終於成書。除提出前開淺見之外，並略述本書之緣起於後，以明始末。

末學於一九八七年初，因執行業務極為繁忙，無時間打坐，每晚課誦金剛經時，總是一面課誦，一面打哈欠，課誦完畢即禮佛菩薩。

是年夏天的某一晚上，課誦完畢拜佛時，忽然想及——應該試著摒除佛號佛相，而以專一憶念佛菩薩之念來禮佛，當下付諸實行。次日起，便都使用無相憶念的禮佛方法。日積月累，細法漸成，竟然熟習無相念佛之法，法喜充滿，渾然不覺世俗生活之忙與累。後來，拜得歡喜，索性停了晚課，專一無相憶念拜佛。日常生活中則專心地無相念佛。

一九八八年底，偶然思及應與大眾分享法喜，乃一方面思索、回憶，將過程逐一記載，一方面閱讀經論以為依據。即將完稿前，翻閱楞嚴經大勢至菩薩念佛圓通章，讀至「憶佛念佛」四字，無限歡喜；而後看到「都攝六根，淨念相繼，入三摩地」，恍然得知此一法門即是大勢至菩薩念佛圓通法門。

隨於一九八九年四月整理記錄，寫成短文，名為「談無相拜佛與無相念佛」。完稿後因閱讀虛雲老和尚之開示錄，始真正摸清了看話頭的理路。方知以前自己以為的參話頭，其實都是在唸話語、看話尾，居然還大言不慚地回答同修道友們，說自己在參話頭。

為何以前不能參話頭，而後來可以呢？原因在於初學時沒有動中的功夫，後來修成無相念佛工夫以後，便有能力參話頭了。

一九八九年八月六日下午，與同參們共修時，兩次進入「見山不是山」的境界，初嚐「黑漆桶」的滋味。此後即常常進出疑團。一九八九年十一月初從印度尼泊爾朝聖回國後，索性歇業，專一在家參禪，直到一九九零年十一月初二下午四時許，黑漆桶兜底粉碎，才結束參禪的歷程。

檢視這一段過程，發覺一般人修習佛法而不得力者，根本原因在於缺乏動中的工夫。因此，寫作此書，希望幫助念佛人迅速修成一心不亂的念佛工夫；並使參禪人早日獲得參話頭、參公案的能力。

末學於一九九一年九月三日起，應共修同參之要求，於台北市某金融機構佛學社之禪修道場及石牌陳居士伉儷之共修禪堂，連續三週講述無相念佛之修持方法（即大勢至菩薩念佛圓通法門之入門方便），共分三次講完。

此二道場同修共約三十人，多數為持名念佛者。他們一面聽聞，一面練習，不過六週，即有二人修成。

三個月屆滿時有六個人修成，至今日（1992.2.28）止，未滿六個月，已有十三人修成。目前仍陸續有人加入，並迅速進步中。比例之高，速度之快，令人鼓舞。而尚無進步消息者，除個人因緣不能拜佛外，主要係因不喜無相憶念拜佛及持名念佛等初期之善巧方便法門，不肯練習所致。及至彼等發覺有不少人陸續修成，並能看話頭參禪時，再急起直追，已遲了三、四個月。

此項實際講述觀察的結果，令末學極為振奮。證實此種法門只要有方便善巧的輔助，和精勤的練習，必能修得。於是再起悲願，所謂不忍聖教衰，不願眾生苦。因此，於寒假中奮筆急書，匆匆寫就。文筆實非典雅，但求信達。平鋪直敘，反復解說。儘量使用白話語句，求其易解。祈願一切有緣的佛弟子，皆可修成無相念佛，普霑法喜，遞相流傳，利益無量無數眾生，同入毗盧性海。

　　南無本師釋迦牟尼世尊
　　南無大悲觀世音菩薩
　　南無大勢至菩薩

三寶弟子蕭平實謹識
公元一九九二年二月二八日

二·《大乘無我觀》序言

　　成佛之道,唯在大乘;二乘菩提無之,二乘聖人不知。二乘菩提唯在蘊處界之觀行上著眼,實修之法,則是四聖諦、八正道、十二因緣法。此等佛法之觀行,則是以四念處為主。然而 世尊在二乘菩提中,已經密意隱說法界之實相,密意隱說無餘涅槃之實際,唯是二乘有學無學諸聖不能了知,故不知爾。逮至迴心大乘時,世尊方令證知,故成大乘法中之大菩薩也。

　　然至法末之季,成佛之道,已然失傳,諸方大師悉已無能知之。若如印順法師著作《成佛之道》一書者,所說之法,實與成佛之道完全無關,完全背離,唯是西藏密宗黃教所傳之應成派中觀爾,本質正是外道斷見之無因論邪見,完全是臆想之戲論,完全悖於成佛之道。

　　成佛之道者,其中心思想乃是一切種智之修證;一切種智之修證者,唯在法界萬法之根本心——第八識實相心蘊含一切種子之智慧。世間及出世間之一切法,都因有情之根本心如來藏體,以及藏識中所蘊藏之無量無數種子,故生五陰、十二處、十八界法,再由此十八界法與如來藏中所含藏之無數種子,輾轉而生十法界一切凡聖萬法;由此十法界一切凡聖萬法,故顯出種種出世間之無為法。由是緣故，說法界之實相，即是眾生本具之自心如來藏——凡夫位中名之為阿賴耶識。

此阿賴耶識，即是中國禪宗證悟者所悟得之第八識真如。然而自古以來，禪宗門中，一向皆有初悟之人，尚未解知成佛之道，隨於錯悟、淺悟之人不實言說，墮於狂禪之中，人云亦云，每言「開悟即是已成究竟佛」，於經中所載已經證悟之諸大菩薩悟已而未成佛之事實，不知檢點，不知探究其故，遂有種種違背佛語之言說，誤導當時及末法今時之學佛人。

凡此過失，皆因不能真實了知禪宗之證悟境界，復又不知在般若智慧之修證上，究竟應如何定位所致。復於三轉法輪之般若修證位階產生誤解、誤判，不知第三轉法輪諸經所開示者，乃是地上菩薩所修證之增上慧學一切種智。復又誤會佛法之道次第，不知成佛之道所應進修之法道次第。復於阿含諸經密意不能證知，隨於印順等誤解阿含諸經意旨者之所說而信受之，故於阿含經旨生諸誤會，便遭密宗應成派中觀邪見之籠罩，隨之步步皆邪，乃至鼎力襄助密宗應成派中觀邪見之弘傳，以此緣故而造下破壞佛教正法之極重惡業，心中猶自以為正在鼎力護持及弘傳佛教正法。

是故，禪宗之真實證悟，固然極為重要；然於禪宗之證悟內涵，及對禪宗之悟在佛法修證上之定位，亦須了知，方免狂禪之弊。知此定位已，則能了知禪宗之證悟，只是大乘般若智慧之初見道而已，尚未能至般若見道之通達位。知此已，則能起心探究悟後進修成佛之道所修證之內涵，則必將漸次探究諸經，而終必進入第三轉法輪諸唯識系經典中，戮力探究成佛之道，則必漸次了知佛道之次第，則可漸次進向初地通達位。至通達位已，則能肩負如來家業,盡形壽破斥邪說而顯正法,復興佛祖家業,成為真佛子住。成初地心已,則能進修及發起更深妙之種智。由有深妙種智故,便能救護一切眾生,悉能破壞佛門中之一切似是而非之邪見,則能導護廣大學人回歸佛教正法之道。則世尊遺法可以無憂也。

　　復次,初地心成就已,亦能了知二乘菩提,能確實宣說二乘菩提所修證之解脫道,則亦能引導學人修證二乘菩提而實證之。實證已,則能令諸佛子發起大心,不畏生死,盡未來際以利眾生。亦能於二乘法之學人,對大乘所作之誤會演說,加以修正,令歸大乘佛法正道。

　　凡此功德之成就,要因禪宗之證悟,以及證悟後進修三賢十聖之大乘無我觀,一一現證其無我觀之境界,而後為人宣演,令諸學人普知大乘法之無我正觀,令知大乘無我觀之異於二乘無我觀之處,則能增益已悟佛子之般若慧,亦能引導學人改變其得自研究佛法而不實修者之研究所得邪見,是故大乘無我觀之內涵,實應令諸佛門學人與證悟者知之,由此緣故,而有此書之出版問世。

　　此書之出版緣起,乃因台南紡織公司侯董事長之邀約,前往台南侯氏宗祠參觀,而引生佛法演示之機緣。此書之內容,即是當天在台南北門鄉侯氏宗祠所作之隨興演講錄音,後來加以整理而出版之。彼時本無演說佛法之計劃,但因接受會中同修之建議,應允作此演講,復因見於大乘佛法道次第不明所衍生之重大影響,故臨時提出此一題目,由來自台南地區之同修們,以此為題而廣告於台南地區,故有這一場佛法聚會。

　　講前並未草書手稿或綱要,亦因事冗,無法撥出時間繕寫綱要,故當時即以閒聊方式,舒適地斜靠於宗祠預備之軟皮椅上,從自心中直接宣演,宣演了將近三小時;復由聞法之大眾當場提出學佛上之疑難問題,當場答覆。但因宗祠之水泥斜屋頂迴音嚴重,又未裝置任何消音板,故使音響產生極大之迴音,導致錄音效果不佳。較嚴重者為:發問者之無線電發訊器未與錄音機連接,故因現場之嚴重迴音,不能清晰錄得發問者之聲音,此是完美法會中之唯一小瑕疵。

演講之錄音帶,經由同修會學員整理成文字後,仍由會員打字完稿,不作修飾,僅將口語稍微理順一些,便直接印行出版,與當時現場所聞者無有絲毫差異,故書中皆是口語化之文辭,未能如一般寫作之顧及典雅,目的僅是在忠實呈現當時之情景以及內涵,作為未來佛教歷史上之見證——藉此顯示今時佛教之蛛絲馬跡。也藉此顯示無遮無隱之佛法般若種智本質,如是利益今時後世廣大學人。茲以此書即將出版,故述緣起,即以此為序。

佛弟子 平實 序於喧囂居
公元二〇〇二年 大暑

三·《真假禪和》前言

　　宗門之證悟，絕對不許外於教門；若有人外於教門聖教之開示，言其所悟「雖異於教門，然亦是宗門之悟」，當知其人即是佛門中之外道，所悟必定已經異於宗門之悟，同於常見外道法，然不能自覺而誤以為悟。

　　一切佛門真修行者皆知如是名言：「從宗出教、從教入宗。」此謂一切真悟者出世弘法，皆是從宗出教；若不是悟入宗門下事，不能如實宣演大乘第一義諦絕妙正理；上自 世尊，中如古今禪宗真悟諸祖，下迄今時一切真悟之人，莫不如是，豈有外於宗門之悟而能如實宣演大乘般若實相甚深之義者？

　　當知一切未悟及錯悟之人宣演大乘般若實相正理時，皆不能外於二相：一者依文解義，不知深義時即言不知，因此不誤導學人；有諸老實弘揚宗門而不敢擅以悟者自居者，可為明證，此為未悟而弘法者之上品人。二者錯解大乘般若諸經正理，但不肯依文解義，故意臆想猜測而誇大其辭妄說禪理，欲令眾人誤以為彼之證量極高；如是諸人多數不免誤導學人乃至否定正法，譬如密宗應成派中觀見之印順、昭慧、性廣法師……等人否定如來藏勝義，可為明證，此是未悟而弘法者之下品人。是故弘揚般若妙義者,當以從宗出教為最殊勝,所說皆能契合實義,不違 世尊及諸大菩薩意旨,並能廣作殊勝妙理之宣揚故。

然而宗門之悟極難,是故佛教歷史上真悟之人,一向皆是極少數,絕非多數。觀乎宗門典籍所載,傳至中土廣為發揚之後,流傳至今亦唯有一千七百則開悟公案而已;其中復有極多錯悟之人,魚目混珠、忝在其中;縱使真悟之人,悟之深淺亦復參差不齊,乃至亦有真心妄心難分難解而致儱侗真如者,如是真妄不分之祖師者所在多有;復因真悟之人迴向往生極樂世界、彌勒淨土、他方諸佛世界者,其數非寡,故此世界真悟祖師再來者不可能日漸增加而無減少者。

又因乘願再來者,一世即有一名號;千餘年來,一人即有二十餘姓名,可知真悟之師一人其實即是往世二十餘祖師名號之代表,但因隔陰之迷而不能知,或因未至捨壽時節故不言之。如是計之,歷代真悟之人必定一向是極少數,由此證明歷代眾多禪師、法師不可能皆是真悟之人:任何時代,絕無可能多數法師、居士皆悟,而只有少數法師、居士未悟。由是可證今時海峽兩岸自稱為悟之人多如過江之鯽者,絕非事實,多屬自以為悟者。復由彼等率皆落入離念靈知意識心境界之事實以觀,亦證實余言之不虛也。如是真相,佛門禪和子們都應知之,以免自誤、誤人,方可保得人身而免下墮,以利世世真修菩薩行;若不知此,錯悟之時卻自以為悟,公然宣稱是證悟聖人,不免因為學禪、修禪之善業而下墮三途,冤枉特甚。

宗門之悟雖然極難,然非決定不能悟,此界必有菩薩受命再來、不令永斷故。若不遇菩薩受命再來者,從教入宗亦是可行之法;雖然多數人從教入宗時不免錯會,猶如今時諸方大師及號稱「導師」之印順法師一般,不免心生邪見、誤會教門，乃至公然誣謗如來藏勝法為外道法。然而此事絕非一定，是故古來多有從教入宗之禪師者，譬如南泉普願禪師、永嘉玄覺禪師、藥山惟儼禪師……等人，皆是從教入宗者，後來皆成宗門下名震當時之一代大禪師。然而從教入宗而悟得宗門下事者，絕非只有禪宗一脈，更有法相唯識宗之玄奘師徒二人，皆入聖位中，非如禪宗多數祖師之唯在三賢位中者；由是緣故即能發起道種智而廣辨法義正邪，令諸方宗門錯悟之師無人能作一語評之，亦令諸方宗門真悟之師不能輕嫌之，唯有取閱進修而崇敬之。

聖玄奘菩薩雖是大乘法師，然於西行求法，未抵西天之前，在西域面見小乘法師木叉毱多時，[32] 已經精通小乘根本論《俱舍論》，故以彼小乘論折伏小乘法師木叉毱多，令其不能再生慢於玄奘菩薩；後始進途西天隨學諸菩薩之大乘論，終令大乘成佛之道妙義及二乘解脫道，因此永立於不敗之地；乃至今日平實亦大受其惠，不敢忘恩，乃造立聖玄奘菩薩像，而與世尊、觀音二尊聖像於正覺同修會第一講堂中並奉而禮拜供養之。是故從教入宗並非絕無僅有，更非絕無可能之事。然而從教入宗者，其所悟內涵亦決不可違背聖教宗旨，否則所說皆成外道戲論，與宗門真旨無關。

如是，宗不離教、教不離宗。世尊因已所悟故，為世人宣說解脫道與佛菩提道，即是從宗出教；世尊所說法語集成文字，流傳人間、久住世間，即成經典；然而如是經典中所說者，皆是宗門下事，不外宗門所悟義理意涵。世人恭閱世尊聖教經典，詳細思惟體究之，一朝緣熟而悟得萬

---

[32] 玄奘在西域所遇見的是木叉毱多，中文原文誤植般若毱多。

法理體之第八識心時，即名從教入宗。**是故宗門與教下本同一源，皆從第八識實相心來**：所悟是第八識實相心，悟後所說則說第八識實相心。由是正理，任何人皆不許妄言「教門異於宗門，教門所說與宗門所悟不同」，若有作是說者，即名凡夫外道邪見，名為不通教門、亦不通宗門之凡夫邪見。宗門祖師常言：「離經一字，即同魔說；依文解義，三世佛冤。」即是此義也！

　　復次，禪宗之悟既屬大乘佛法，則必有果可判：或成究竟佛，或為等覺菩薩，或為諸地菩薩，或為三賢菩薩乃至十信位菩薩。若屬二乘解脫道之修法，亦必有果可判：或成辟支佛果，或成三明六通大阿羅漢，或為俱解脫阿羅漢，或為慧解脫阿羅漢，或為三果、二果、初果聖人。如是三乘菩提之修證，無一不可判果者。若言宗門之悟不攝在三乘菩提之果位中，乃至狂言一悟即至佛地而主張不能判其果位者，則彼成佛之果位是否不攝佛法證量果位？若然，即非成佛，即成「外道佛」，所悟皆不攝在佛法果證中故；若所悟是佛法所攝者，則必攝在成佛階次之五十二階位中，焉可說其悟境無果可判？是故一切佛法中之修行者，所證般若境界無一不可判果者；其判果者，要在如實而判，不依增上慢心而作妄判，方是真修佛法之人也！若不知應判何果，若不能自判其果，則其人顯然無智自驗，尚不能自知所處果位名目，焉知悟後如何進修增上佛法、漸次邁向佛地？則成狂慧無智之愚人也！空言一悟成佛，究竟有何實質意義？宗門一切禪和，對此皆應具有正見，方免自誤而又誤人，貽患後身。

　　復次，成佛固以宗門初悟第八識真如心為基礎，方可漸次進修而成就究竟佛道，是故宗門初悟所得根本無分別智（即是華嚴及起信論所說之阿賴耶識本覺智），實是成佛法道之入門；若不能悟得宗門第八識本覺智勝法，則不入此門，即無成佛之道可言。然而入門之後，如何次第漸修而後真能成佛？實言之：端賴一切種智。

　　明言之：十方法界一切佛土諸佛，無有不得一切種智而能成佛者；諸大阿羅漢之所以不能成佛，咎在未證第八識本覺智般若；諸大菩薩尚未能成佛者，咎在一切種智尚未具足圓滿；故說一切種智即是成佛之根本，不具足一切種智者永不能成佛。然而一切種智之義理內涵，今時竟然無人知之；乃至一切種智所依理體之第八識如來藏，竟敢公然否定之。如是不證一切種智所依理體之第八識如來藏，不證如來藏所含藏之一切種子內涵，不證一切種智，竟敢公然主張其錯認為真如心之意識心即是實相心，而且公然主張宗門與教門無關，又公然將成佛唯一法門之唯識門一切種智增上慧學，判在般若總相智、別相智之下；然而一切種智乃是悟入般若總相智、別相智以後，方能修學之增上慧學，彼等卻因自己未能修證故，便判在般若總相智與別相智之下；乃至將唯識一切種智判在宗門錯悟者落入意識生滅法之凡夫見解以下，其妄乃爾，殊不可與語。由是緣故，正德居士不得不以大量開示解說，詳細辨正之，其老婆心切溢於言表，致有此書鉅大篇幅問世，欲令宗門廣大禪和普獲其利。茲以此書出版在即，邀序於余，即以略述法理及緣起，以代序言。

佛子 平實敬序
時值二〇〇五年初春

四·《狂密與真密》選錄

　　然而　佛於三乘諸經中，皆說一切眾生之法身即是其本有之第八識體，此識之體無始以來法爾本有，圓滿具足，非因修集諸種子所成，非因修集諸種子而有。於大品小品般若諸經中，佛又名之為「非心心、無心相心、不念心、無住心、菩薩心⋯⋯」。佛又說此無始本有之法身，具足無量種子，法爾而有一切無漏有漏種子；由有如是法爾而有之無漏有漏種子，是故佛子能因如是法爾而有之無漏種子而修成佛地功德。

------《狂密與真密》一，頁289

　　復次，顯教諸經中，一向皆說真心如來藏——第八識阿賴耶識——體恒、不生不滅，無始本有；又復處處說此第八識真心一向遠離見聞覺知⋯⋯。

------《狂密與真密》一，頁291-292

　　密宗內之古今諸師，每將佛法義理擅以己意而解釋之，不肯依經中正義而探究之，致令法義紊亂無章、令己及他皆入歧途；復又引入外道所修氣功明點⋯⋯諸法，擅以自

意搭配佛法修證之名相,而言果證,故皆入於外道邪見之中,非是佛教所言所修所證之法也。

當知阿賴耶識不唯是眾生輪迴常住三界之因,亦是一切聖者所證涅槃之因。不迴心於大乘之定性聲聞阿羅漢,由修證解脫道故,斷除我見我執已,捨壽時滅盡十八界法,不復有意根末那識出現,故其第八識由其本性「恒不思量了別作主」,而不再受生三界之中,名為無餘涅槃;末那識已滅而不復現行故,無有一心能引第八識受生入胎故。

如是入無餘涅槃者,唯是第八識獨存,不復有見聞覺知心現行,不觸六塵,故曰「涅槃寂靜」;亦無末那識之思量心性現行,復無前六識之了知心性現行,故無七轉識之心行,遠離「諸行無常」,一切見聞覺知之心行及末那識之思量心行悉滅故;如是無餘涅槃名為真實無我,前七識之見聞覺知性及思量作主性皆已滅盡故,而第八識如來藏自體一向離見聞覺知及思量作主性,故無「我性」可得、故無「我性」現行,不墮「諸法無我」所破之外道「我性」之中;如是而符三法印,方是真實無餘涅槃也。

由是可知第八識阿賴耶正是眾生修證涅槃之根本因,涅槃以第八識為體故,離第八識則無涅槃可修可證故,離第八識則無餘涅槃即成斷滅故……。

------《狂密與真密》一,頁293-294

密宗諸師多以一切法空為法身,非以第八識為法身……密宗所說之一切法空者,則是以覺知心與明點獨自存在,而不觀想一切諸法,不令一切諸法出現,名為一切法空;如是覺知心與明點獨存而不出現其餘所觀之法,名為一切法空之「法身」。若依於明點而觀想其餘諸法變生而出者,即是前六識之現境功能,名為「化身」。若覺知心於

此明點境界之中，有其明性（了知性）存在而不生染著性者，其覺知心之明性即是「報身」。

……所說不符三乘法義故，違背龍樹菩薩所造之諸多論述意旨故；乃是密宗祖師以自意解釋法身，謂覺知心於明點現量境界上現行時，不起分別及貪著瞋痴等，則此時之覺知心即是「一切法空之法身」也。如是以覺知心為法身已，謂法身覺知心有明性（於一念不生時而能了知六塵之分別性）。……然實覺知心乃所生之緣起法，即是前六識，不具顯現境界之功能，亦非化身，六識所了知境乃是內相分，悉由第八識前現故。

------《狂密與真密》一，頁294-296

縱使能令覺知心於二六時中皆住於一念不生之狀態中而不昏沉及眠夢，如是保持一生而不眠夢，仍不能改變其意識之本質。假饒能令覺知心常處於一念不生之境，連續三劫五劫，仍然是意識，無改於彼意識之本質。意識永遠是意識，乃至成就究竟佛地之修行，意識仍是意識，仍不能變成佛地之真如──第十無垢識。是故密宗欲將意識常處於一念不生之境，而轉變意識為佛地真如者，乃是妄想；如是修行，非佛法之正修也。依之而修三大無量數劫之後，他人已經成佛已，密宗諸人之不肯轉入顯教而修者，仍將繼續處於凡夫位而自以為已證佛果，三大無量數劫之修行，悉皆徒勞無功也。

------《狂密與真密》一，頁299

五・《宗門道眼》選錄

　　悟道之最速者莫過於禪宗，教人悟道而最具成績者亦莫過於禪宗；(如今為佛教末法時期)，想要在東密西密(藏密)中欲覓一位真悟道者，極難可得，不道古代難得，現代亦復不得。

　　　　　　　　　　　　------《宗門道眼》，頁177

　　大乘佛教則腳踏實地，按部就班，次第而進。每一階段皆可自行依經尋論而印證之，非如密宗之未修未證，而以鬼神所示及錯誤諸祖之自我吹噓而作不實之果位名目印證。

　　　　　　　　　　　　------《宗門道眼》，頁211

　　奉勸佛子欲求速成佛道者，當求大乘見道——破參明心。莫隨藏密諸師於外門修學佛法。更莫修學無上瑜伽雙身修法，此是印度教之行門，與夜叉、辟荔相應；破財失身事小，犯戒破法事大，萬勿輕忽。若欲速入大乘見道位，禪宗之禪最為迅速，一念相應便入相似即佛位；若有福德善根，一生可修入初地……。

　　　　　　　　　　　　------《宗門道眼》，頁211

無明即是愚癡，佛法中所說無明愚痴，乃說有情不明空性實相，故大乘諸經說：輪迴三界之有情為凡夫，二乘無學聖人為愚痴。以不明空性實相故，說二乘聖人為愚；合三界凡夫，名為凡愚。不瞭解、誤解、誤會、及懷疑空性實相，皆名為愚；故二乘無學雖出三界，仍名為愚。

-----《宗門道眼》，頁274

　　禪之開悟，不可用觀心得，未悟之前尚不知真心何在，何有真心可觀？故不可用觀心之法求悟，當以覓心之法求悟。覓心之前應先了知有情無念靈知心之虛妄，於此靈知心外另覓同時存在之非見聞覺知心，是故參禪不可用觀心之法，當用覓心之法，尋覓無始劫來不曾現起三界覺知之真心。覓心之法無如參話頭與參公案。

------《宗門道眼》，頁36

　　興化存獎禪師為唐莊宗之師。一日莊宗謂師曰：「朕收大梁，得一顆無價明珠，未有人酬價。」「請陛下珠看。」帝以手舒開幞頭之腳，師曰：「君王之寶，誰敢酬價？」玄覺禪師聽到這個公案，便問諸方老前輩：「你們請說說看，興化禪師這個答話，是肯定莊宗有悟？還是不肯？如果是肯定的話，請問：興化的法眼在什麼處？如果是不肯的話，莊宗皇帝的過失在何處？」

　　千年後，平實代興化答他莊宗一句：「恰值一天下！」且道平實此語肯不肯莊宗？若肯莊宗，因何道他恰好值得一天下？若不肯莊宗，因何又道他值得一天下？且道平實意在何處？

------《宗門道眼》，頁183

創古仁波切云:「意識必定是在子宮受孕之前就已經存在了,因此,在此之前必定有生世。就以今天我們能覺知並具有意識的事實來說吧!這是否表示也許明天心將不復存在,你將沒有心?不,事情並不是這樣。不論身與心之間的連繫是否中斷了,意識的連續性仍然存在。基於這種邏輯,我們可以確定未來世的存在,沒有任何現象可以阻斷這種意識的連續性。這是佛陀所教示的,並為佛教所有不同學派所接受。」

　　平實云:仁波切此段開示,正與佛陀教示相反,並為大多數學派所反對,只有應成派中觀師認同。此謂覺知者(意識)日日斷滅,依賴等無間緣方能與昨日之意識連接而憶昨日事。醒後之意識亦是念念變易生滅,猶如影片之每一格引導後一格現前,即是前一刹那意識種子落謝前,開避其位,引導後一刹那意識種子繼於其位現行,連續不斷生滅替代,方能成就意識之明與覺知體性,故明與覺知是念念生滅不住之體性;意識若斷,明與覺知隨滅。

　　然意識有三種俱有依——末那及阿賴耶識與五勝義根(不是自己本來存在者)。此方是 佛陀所說,方是所有佛教宗派所接受者。意識既須有此三俱有依,則末那(意根)不欲其現行時,意識即不能現行;如入二無心定中及眠熟時,意識不能現行運作,無覺無知。若無阿賴耶識執藏意識種子,末那雖欲意識現行覺知,亦不能令意識覺知現起;如人(意根)欲令水龍頭之水流出(使覺知的現象現行),而水塔中無水(譬如阿賴耶識中無存意識種子),則人(意根)不能令水流出;已流出之水不能憑空令水塔自行生水故,意識亦然,已出現之意識不能自生下一念意識。前一念意識不能產生下一念意識,須由阿賴耶識所儲藏之意識種子源源不斷踵接其位而現,方能成就意識之覺知及明了作用;密宗一向服膺《慈氏五論》,而彌勒菩薩已於《瑜伽師地論》詳論此義,仁波切未聞未讀之耶?抑或讀而不解耶?竟謂「前一剎那意識能生後一剎那意識」。

意識復依五勝義根方能現起,若五勝義根壞死(如大腦壞死),意識便不現行而永斷滅,明覺永不復現。若全身麻醉,五勝義根(大腦)不能運作,則意識覺知亦中斷。此諸正理,人盡皆知,云何仁波切為「人中寶」,而竟不知?

二者仁波切認為意識是在子宮受孕之前就已存在,並認為此世之意識覺知是由前世延續而來,實違佛說及菩薩說;若真如此,則應人人皆具報得宿命通,不須加修宿命通而後能知前世事。亦應人人皆能正知入胎、正知住胎、正知出胎,前世之意識不滅而入胎住胎出胎故;則仁波切應能記憶前世如何入胎、此世如何住胎、於胎中亦應有睡眠時及覺知明了時,亦應正知出胎;而現見仁波切及一切未具宿命通之有情悉皆不能如此。故知意識須依當世之五根和意根(末那)及阿賴耶識方能現行,若缺其一,即告中斷,故知此世意識須依此色身大腦(五根勝義根)之漸漸具足而由無至有、由微至顯,非初入胎時即有意識覺知也。五根壞已,當世之意識永斷,不去至來生,唯有阿賴耶識執藏此世意識種子及業種,依業依願隨末那受於來生。此諸正理明載經論之中,方是佛所教示,方是大乘各學派所共認者;唯有應成中觀師認同宗喀巴之邪見,否定末那及阿賴耶,錯執「意識不生滅,可以去至來世,為一切法所依」(詳見宗喀巴著《入中論善顯密意疏、辨了不了義善說藏論》),違逆佛及慈氏教示,否定正法根本,云何名為佛教?

若意識恆不生滅,則意識不能成就其明了覺知之作用,此理已於《真實如來藏》中詳述;若意識永不斷滅,則應明了覺知之性恆時現行不斷,則應一切人眠熟、悶覺、入無想定及滅盡定、正死位中,皆悉明了覺知自己正在眠熟悶覺等狀況中,則應無此五法,謂佛說意識於此五位皆滅而不現故。仁波切之開示者,不唯違教,亦且悖理,云何以此邪謬知見以度眾生?此名誤導眾生也!

仁波切欲離此邪見者,唯有親自實證空性阿賴耶識,方能了知密宗四大派諸祖及應成中觀師之邪謬;且舉白雲鞋袋公案,共仁波切商量:

> 韶州白雲實性大師一日上堂對大眾開示:「你們大家會不會空性?只須向街頭市尾那些殺豬切肉等地獄熱湯處去體會。如果是這樣體會來的人,才可以當人家的師父,為人雕琢;如果是在寺院中向衲僧們修學來的,可就天地懸殊了。更一類人,只向禪堂長連床上打坐,不幹惡事;你們說說看:這兩種人,哪一個有長處?沒事的話,大家便下去休息吧!」

> 白雲禪師問一僧云:「你從何處來?」僧答:「從雲門來。」白雲又問:「雲門之內有多少頭水牛?(問有多少人開悟也)?」僧答:「有一個兩個。」白雲禪師讚云:「好水牛。」讚已復問:「不捨世間假相及名言,而譚真如實相,你怎麼說祂?」僧答:「這個是椅子。」白雲禪師以手撥推彼僧云:「取我的鞋袋來!」彼僧不知所措。後來雲門禪師聞說此一公案便云:「須是白雲禪師才能如此啊!」

只如古今諸大道場開法度眾,教令座下眾僧打坐參禪者甚眾,白雲禪師因什麼道理不許?反教座下眾僧向街頭殺豬宰羊處會取?此處乃是傍生有情之現地獄,斧鉞鑊湯,殘忍已極,有何可取?而教遠離葷腥之眾僧向彼臊臭處會取？然而平實仍勸仁波切向此處會取空性真如，莫閉目觀想空行母及本尊等，此是凡夫所行禪，妄想之自境，無關第一義諦；若如是觀者，窮劫亦不見道。

仁波切若肯向西藏殺羊宰牛處會取，一眼撇見空性如來藏後，即可永見此空性心常駐有情蘊處界中，永不退失見地，唯除信慧不足而自我否定者。仁波切這一覷得，便能檢點藏密四大派諸祖之邪謬，正好邁向全球諸大道場，令弟子們回西藏印度鄉下街頭看殺牛宰羊去！個個盡成獅子兒，向天下哮吼——摧邪顯正；則密教從此脫胎換骨，佛法大興也。

白雲禪師一日問僧：「什麼處來？」彼僧答云：「雲門來。」若是伶俐漢，未答訖，便合省悟，就地禮他白雲禪師。白雲仁慈，卻不打他，更待機緣，乃問：「雲門有多少悟者？」僧答：「一個兩個。」白雲曰：「好水牛。」此便難會。白雲見他機遲，索性入水和泥，敞明了問：「不壞假名而譚實相，你作麼生說？」彼僧從各處學得皮毛，便拿來試試手氣：「這個是椅子。」平實若在，當時取椅丟出門外云：「這個不是椅子！」喚作啐啄同時。白雲卻突出奇峰，以手撥推彼僧云：「把鞋袋子取過來！」彼僧若是個具福慧底，聞言取過鞋袋呈上時，恰好直下會去！無奈他不知所措。平實若在，便大聲斥云：「取鞋袋子也不會！」無奈彼僧毛羽未具，白雲遂鈍置他。雲門禪師後來聞道此個公案，便嘆云：「須是白雲禪師方能如此啊！」可見當時諸大禪師中野狐甚眾，雲門方有此語，謂諸師不解白雲弄蛇手段也。

只如仁波切千里迢迢，遠從印北來到台灣寶島；既是寶島，當有無上正法大寶在此，仁波切回時切莫空手而歸；入寶山而空手回，令人恥笑。仁波切切莫令人笑，當速向寶島中到處會取。若會不得,來覓平實;且邀正覺講堂相見,見時平實便喚:「仁波切!」上座答諾;若仍機遲,平實便教:「脫下皮鞋,入講堂去!」入得講堂若猶不會,堪作什麼?

------《宗門道眼》,頁313 - 318

Chart: The Cultivation Stages within the Two Main Paths of Buddha Bodhi
(English & Chinese)

The Cultivation Stages of the Two Paths within the Buddha Bodhi

The joint cultivation of these two paths is the one and only way to attain Buddhahood

		The Great Bodhi: Path to Buddhahood		The Bodhi of the Two Lesser Vehicles: Path to Liberation
Distant Pāramitās	Path of Accumulation	Ten Faiths: Bodhisattvas accumulate faith in the Buddha Dharma. This will take one to ten thousand eons to accomplish.	Extensively practicing the six *pāramitās* before achieving awakening to the True Mind.	
		First Abiding: Bodhisattvas accumulate virtues of charitable giving, primarily material goods.		Practitioners eliminate the three fetters to attain the first fruition of liberation.
		Second Abiding: Bodhisattvas accumulate virtues of precept observance.		
		Third Abiding: Bodhisattvas accumulate virtues of forbearance.		
		Fourth Abiding: Bodhisattvas accumulate virtues of diligence.		
		Fifth Abiding: Bodhisattvas accumulate virtues of meditative absorption.		
		Sixth Abiding: Bodhisattvas accumulate virtues of *prajñā*, by studying and familiarizing themselves with the Middle Way of *prajñā* and eliminating the view of self during the Path of Preparation.		
▲ First Faith to Tenth Dedication	Path of Vision	Seventh Abiding: Bodhisattvas awaken to the True Mind and gain direct comprehension of *prajñā*, thereupon realize directly the nirvana with primordial, intrinsic and pure nature.	Extensively practicing the six *pāramitās* after achieving awakening to the True Mind.	Practitioners attain the second fruition of liberation by reducing greed, aversion, and delusion.
		Eighth Abiding: Starting from this stage, bodhisattvas gain direct comprehension of the Middle Way of *prajñā* in all phenomena, and gradually eliminate their dispositional hindrances.		
		Tenth Abiding: Bodhisattvas see the Buddha-nature with the physical eye and attain direct comprehension of the illusoriness of the world.		
		First Practice to Tenth Practice: While extensively cultivating the six *pāramitās*, bodhisattvas rely on their insights into the Middle Way of *prajñā* to directly comprehend the aggregates, sense-fields, and elements are illusory like mirages. Upon completing the Tenth Practice, they will have fully accomplished the direct comprehension of these phenomena being like mirages.		Practitioners attain the third fruition of liberation by eliminating the five lower fetters.
		First Dedication to Tenth Dedication: Bodhisattvas study and familiarize themselves with the knowledge-of-all-aspects and eliminate dispositional hindrances, except the last bit of affliction eradicated through cultivation. Upon completing the Tenth Dedication, they will have attained direct comprehension of the bodhisattva path being like a dream.		

		Near Pāramitās ▲ First Ground to Seventh Ground	
Path of Vision	First Ground: Upon completing the Tenth Dedication, bodhisattvas will have realized a portion of the knowledge-of-the-aspects-of-paths, consisting of personal and direct realization of each of the eight consciousnesses, which enables them to perceive the five aspects of dharmas, the three natures, the seven intrinsic natures [of the *tathāgatagarbha*], and the two types of selflessness. They enter the Stage of Proficiency (First Ground) after bravely making the ten inexhaustible vows. Also, they have forever subdued the dispositional hindrances without eliminating them completely. While they can attain liberation from samsara through wisdom at this point, they purposely retain the last bit of afflictive hindrances to nourish future rebirths out of their great vows. The principal cultivation of the First Ground consists of the *pāramitā* of Dharma teaching as well as the Hundred Dharmas. The cultivation of the First Ground is completed when bodhisattvas attain direct comprehension of the six sense-objects being like images in a mirror.		Before entering the First Ground, bodhisattvas undertake four levels of intensified efforts to eradicate the manifestation of all afflictive hindrances and attain the fourth fruition of liberation. However, the last bit of afflictive hindrances is purposely retained to nourish future rebirths. Bodhisattvas have put an end to delimited existence (*paricchedajarāmaraṇa*) and proceed to eliminate the habitual seeds of afflictive hindrances, as well as the higher afflictions of beginningless ignorance.
Path of Cultivation	Second Ground: Bodhisattvas enter the Second Ground when they have completed their cultivation of the First Ground and realized an additional portion of the knowledge-of-the-aspects-of-paths. Cultivation of this stage focuses on the *pāramitā* of precept observance and the knowledge-of-all-aspects. Upon completing the Second Ground, bodhisattvas will have attained direct comprehension of the first seven consciousnesses being like light and shadows. Thereupon, they will be able to adhere to precepts in a way that is both pure and natural.		
	Third Ground: Bodhisattvas advance to the Third Ground after having realized an additional portion of the knowledge-of-the-aspects-of-paths upon completing the Second Ground. The principal cultivation of the Third Ground includes the *pāramitā* of forbearance, the four concentrations and the four formless absorptions, the four boundless minds, as well as the five supernatural powers. While bodhisattvas on the Third Ground can realize the fruition of twofold liberation, they deliberately choose not to; instead, they purposely retain the last bit of afflictive hindrances to nourish future rebirths. Upon completing the Third Ground, bodhisattvas will have attained direct comprehension of all voices of Dharma teaching being like echoes in a valley and achieved the mind-made body attained through the taintless and wondrous *samādhi*.		
	Fourth Ground: Bodhisattvas advance to the Fourth Ground after having realized an additional portion of the knowledge-of-the-aspects-of-paths on the Third Ground. The principal cultivation of this stage is the *pāramitā* of diligence, for which bodhisattvas extensively and tirelessly teach and guide sentient beings who have karmic connections with them in this and other worlds. They will also continue their cultivation of the knowledge-of-all-aspects. Upon completing the Fourth Ground, bodhisattvas will have attained direct comprehension of their own mind-made bodies generated during *samādhi* being like the moon reflected in water.		
	Fifth Ground: Bodhisattvas advance to the Fifth Ground after having realized an additional portion of the knowledge-of-the-aspects-of-paths on the Fourth Ground. The *pāramitā* of meditative absorption and the knowledge-of-all-aspects constitute the principal cultivation of the Fifth Ground. Bodhisattvas will also eliminate the desire for nirvana possessed by adherents of the lesser vehicles. Upon completing the Fifth Ground, they will have attained direct comprehension of all bodhisattvas' mind-made bodies and emanation bodies being like the effects of conjuring.		

Near Pāramitās ▲	Path of Cultivation	Sixth Ground: Bodhisattvas advance to the Sixth Ground after having realized an additional portion of the knowledge-of-the-aspects-of-paths on the Fifth Ground. The principal cultivation of the Sixth Ground is the *pāramitā* of *prajñā*: relying on the knowledge-of-the-aspects-of-paths they have acquired, bodhisattvas directly comprehend that each of the twelve factors of dependent arising as well as the mind-made and emanation bodies are all transformations of one's mind of True Suchness, and therefore are "seemingly but not truly existent." Having accomplished the contemplation of the subtle characteristics of these dharmas, they acquire the ability to spontaneously realize the meditative absorption of cessation without any added effort. Thereupon, they become Mahāyāna adepts (*aśaikṣa*) of twofold liberation.	Upon completing the Seventh Ground, bodhisattvas will have eliminated the last bit of "affliction eradicated through cultivation" that has been purposely retained. They will also have thoroughly eliminated all tainted habitual seeds of afflictive hindrances associated with the aggregates of form, sensation, and perception.
First Ground to Seventh Ground		Seventh Ground: After attaining direct comprehension of the transformations of one's own mind of True Suchness being "seemingly but not truly existent" on the Sixth Ground, bodhisattvas attain an additional portion of the knowledge-of-the-aspects-of-paths and advance to the Seventh Ground. The cultivation of the Seventh Ground focuses on continued learning of the knowledge-of-all-aspects and the *pāramitā* of skillful means. Additionally, bodhisattvas contemplate again all the subtle characteristics of each of the twelve factors of dependent arising from the perspectives of transmigration and the extinction of transmigration, whereby they achieve mastery of skillful means and the ability to enter the meditative absorption of cessation in a single thought. Upon completing the Seventh Ground, bodhisattvas will have attained direct comprehension of the nirvana they have realized being as illusory as a *gandharva's* city.	
Great Pāramitās ▲ **Eighth Ground to Virtual Enlightenment**		Eighth Ground: Having attained the contemplation of the extremely subtle characteristics on the Seventh Ground, bodhisattvas realize an additional portion of the knowledge-of-the-aspects-of-paths and advance to the Eighth Ground. The principal cultivation of the Eighth Ground concentrates on the continued learning of the knowledge-of-all-aspects and the *pāramitā* of vows. Upon completing the Eighth Ground, bodhisattvas will be able to spontaneously bring forth the exclusively signless contemplation at all times and hence can manipulate physical objects or mental images at will. Also, they will have realized the mind-made body attained through correct realization of dharma characteristics.	Bodhisattvas gradually and spontaneously eliminate the taintless habitual seeds of afflictive hindrances associated with the aggregates of formation and consciousness, as well as the higher afflictions of cognitive hindrances.
		Ninth Ground: Bodhisattvas advance to the Ninth Ground after having realized an additional portion of the knowledge-of-the-aspects-of-paths on the Eighth Ground. The principal cultivation of the Ninth Ground consists of the *pāramitā* of strength as well as continued learning of the knowledge-of-all-aspects. Upon completing the Ninth Ground, bodhisattvas will have mastered the four unhindered knowledges and realized the mind-made body attained without added effort and in accordance with the classes of beings to be delivered.	
		Tenth Ground: Bodhisattvas advance to the Tenth Ground after having realized an additional portion of the knowledge-of-the-aspects-of-paths on the Ninth Ground. The principal cultivation of the Tenth Ground is the knowledge-of-all-aspects, namely, the *pāramitā* of omniscience. Upon completing the Tenth Ground, bodhisattvas will be able to generate the cloud of great Dharma wisdom and manifest the various meritorious qualities contained therein. They will also become a "designated bodhisattva."	

Great Pāramitās	Path of Cultivation	Virtual Enlightenment: After having realized the portion of the knowledge-of-the-aspects-of-paths cultivated on the Tenth Ground, bodhisattvas advance to the stage of Virtual Enlightenment. At this stage, they cultivate the knowledge-of-all-aspects and perfectly realize the acquiescence to the non-arising of dharmas (*anutpattikadharmakṣānti*) pertaining to this stage. They will also perfect the thirty-two majestic physical features and immumerable associated good marks unique to Buddha by cultivating and accumulating enormous amount of virtues over a hundred eons.	Bodhisattvas gradually and spontaneously eliminate the taintless habitual seeds of afflictive hindrances associated with the aggregates of formation and consciousness, as well as the higher afflictions of cognitive hindrances.
Perfect Pāramitās	Path of Ultimate Realization	Sublime Enlightenment: Bodhisattvas have thoroughly eliminated all habitual seeds of afflictive hindrances and all latent cognitive hindrances, as well as permanently eradicated the ignorance that leads to transformational existence. They will manifest birth in the human world, realize the great nirvana, and perfect the four kinds of wisdom of Buddha. After displaying physical death in the human world, their reward-bodies will permanently reside in the highest heaven of the form-realm to continue to teach and guide bodhisattvas on or above the First Ground coming from all worlds. Having accomplished the ultimate fruition of Buddhahood, they will generate numerous emanation bodies to perpetually teach and guide sentient beings.	Bodhisattvas bring transformational existence (*parinamikijarāmaraṇa*) to a complete end and attain the great nirvana.

Perfect Ultimate Fruition of Buddhahood
Respectfully composed by Buddhist disciple Xiao Pingshi (Feb. 2012)

佛菩提二主要道次第概要表
二道並修，以外無別佛法

		佛菩提道——大菩提道		解脫道：二乘菩提
資糧位		十信位修集信心——一劫乃至一萬劫。		
		初住位修集布施功德（以財施為主）。		
		二住位修集持戒功德。		
		三住位修集忍辱功德。		
		四住位修集精進功德。		
		五住位修集禪定功德。		
見道位		六住位修集般若功德（薰習般若中觀及斷我見，加行位也。）	外門廣修六度萬行	斷三縛結，成初果解脫
		七住位明心般若正觀現前，親證本來自性清淨涅槃。		
		八住位起於一切法現觀般若中道。漸除性障。		
		十住位眼見佛性，世界如幻觀成就。		
		一至十行位，於廣行六度萬行中，依般若中道慧，現觀陰處界猶如陽焰，至第十行滿心位，陽焰觀成就。	內門廣修六度萬行	薄貪瞋癡，成二果解脫
		一至十迴向位熏習一切種智；消除性障，唯留最後一分思惑不斷。第十迴向滿心位成就菩薩道如夢觀。		斷五下分結，成三果解脫
遠波羅蜜多：初信至十迴向				

見道位	初地：第十迴向位滿心時，成就道種智一分（八識心王——親證三自性，三種道，七種第一義，二種無我法）後，領受五法，成滿達位菩薩。復由勇發十無盡願，由大願故留惑潤生，慧解脫而不取證。此地主修法施波羅蜜多及百法明門。證「猶如鏡像」現觀，故滿初地心。	入地前的四加行令煩惱障現行悉斷，成四果解脫，留惑潤生。分段生死已斷，煩惱障習氣種子開始斷除，兼斷無始無明上煩惱。
修道位	二地：初地功德滿足以後，再成就道種智一分而入二地。主修戒波羅蜜多及一切種智。滿心位成就「猶如光影」現觀，戒行自然清淨。	
	三地：二地滿心再證道種智一分，故入三地。此地主修忍波羅蜜多及四禪八定、四無量心、五神通。能成就俱解脫果而不取證，留惑潤生。滿心位成就「猶如谷響」現觀及無漏妙定意生身。	
	四地：由三地再證道種智一分故入四地。主修精進波羅蜜多。於此土及他方世界廣度有緣，無有疲倦。進修一切種智，滿心位成就「如水中月」現觀。	
	五地：由四地再證道種智一分故入五地。主修禪定波羅蜜多及一切種智，斷除下乘涅槃貪。滿心位成就「變化所成」現觀。	
	六地：由五地再證道種智一分故入六地。此地主修般若波羅蜜多——依道種智現觀十二因緣一一有支及意生身化身，皆自心真如變化所現，「非有似有」，成就細相觀，不由加行而自然證得滅盡定，成俱解脫大乘無學。	
	七地：由六地「非有似有」現觀，再證道種智一分故入七地。此地主修一切種智及方便波羅蜜多，由重觀十二有支一一支中之流轉門及還滅門一切細相，成就方便善巧，念念隨入滅盡定。滿心位證得「如犍闥婆城」現觀。	七地滿心斷除故意保留之最後一分思惑時，煩惱障所攝色、受、想三陰有漏習氣種子同時斷盡。

近波羅蜜多：初地至七地

大波羅蜜多：八地至等覺	修道位	八地：由七地極細相觀成就故再證道種智一分而入八地。此地主修一切種智及顯波羅蜜多，至滿心位復證「如實知諸法相意生身」故。滿心位純無相觀任運恆起，故於相土自在，滿心位復證「如實知諸法相意生身」。	煩惱障所攝行、識二陰無漏習氣種子任運漸斷，所知障所攝上煩惱任運漸斷。
		九地：由八地再證道種智一分故入九地。主修力波羅蜜多及一切種智，成就四無礙，滿心位證得「種類俱生無行作意生身」。	
		十地：由九地再證道種智一分故入此地。此地主修一切種智——智波羅蜜多。滿心位起大法智雲，及現起大法智雲所含藏種種功德，成受職菩薩。	
		等覺：由十地道種智成就故入此地。此地應修一切種智，圓滿等覺地無生法忍；於百劫中修集極廣大福德，以之圓滿三十二大人相及無量隨形好。	
圓滿波羅蜜多	究竟位	妙覺：示現受生人間已斷盡煩惱障一切習氣種子，並斷盡所知障一切隨眠，永斷變易生死無明，成就大般涅槃，四智圓明，人間捨壽後，報身常住色究竟天利樂十方地上菩薩；以諸化身利樂有情，永無盡期，成就究竟佛道。	斷盡變易生死，成就大般涅槃。

圓 滿 成 就 究 竟 佛 果
佛子蕭平實 謹製 (2012年2月)

Cultivation Centers of the True Enlightenment Practitioners Association

Taipei True Enlightenment Lecture Hall
9F, No. 277, Sec. 3, Chengde Rd., Taipei 103, Taiwan, R.O.C.
Tel.: +886-2-2595-7295
(Ext. 10 & 11 for 9F; 15 & 16 for 10F; 18 & 19 for 5F; and 14 for the bookstore on 10F.)

Daxi True Enlightenment Patriarch Hall
No. 5-6, Kengdi, Ln. 650, Xinyi Rd., Daxi Township, Taoyuan County 335, Taiwan, R.O.C.
Tel.: +886-3-388-6110

Taoyuan True Enlightenment Lecture Hall
10F, No. 286 & 288, Jieshou Rd., Taoyuan 330, Taiwan, R.O.C.
Tel.: +886-3-374-9363

Hsinchu True Enlightenment Lecture Hall
2F-1, No. 55, Dongguang Rd., Hsinchu 300, Taiwan, R.O.C.
Tel.: +886-3-572-4297

Taichung True Enlightenment Lecture Hall
13F-4, No. 666, Sec. 2, Wuquan W. Rd., Nantun Dist., Taichung 408, Taiwan, R.O.C.
Tel.: +886-4-2381-6090

Jiayi True Enlightenment Lecture Hall
8F-1, No. 288, Youai Rd., Jiayi 600, Taiwan, R.O.C.
Tel.: +886-5-231-8228

Tainan True Enlightenment Lecture Hall
4F, No. 15, Sec. 4, Ximen Rd., Tainan 700, Taiwan, R.O.C.
Tel.: +886-6-282-0541

Kaohsiung True Enlightenment Lecture Hall
5F, No. 45, Zhongzheng 3rd Rd., Kaohsiung 800, Taiwan, R.O.C.
Tel.: +886-7-223-4248

Los Angeles True Enlightenment Lecture Hall
825 S. Lemon Ave, Diamond Bar, CA 91789, U.S.A.
Tel.: +1-909-595-5222
Cell: +1-626-454-0607

Hong Kong True Enlightenment Lecture Hall
Unit E1, 27th Floor, TG Place, 10 Shing Yip Street, Kwun Tong, **Kowloon, Hong Kong**
Tel: +852-2326-2231

Website of the True Enlightenment Practitioners Association:
http://www.enlighten.org.tw

Website of the True Wisdom Publishing Co.:
http://books.enlighten.org.tw

Readers may download free publications of the Association from the above website.

www.ingramcontent.com/pod-product-compliance
Lightning Source LLC
Chambersburg PA
CBHW070243100426
42743CB00011B/2105